LONG NIGHT AT THE VEPSIAN MUSEUM

LONG NIGHT AT THE VEPSIAN MUSEUM

THE FOREST FOLK OF NORTHERN RUSSIA AND THE STRUGGLE FOR CULTURAL SURVIVAL

VERONICA DAVIDOV

UNIVERSITY OF TORONTO PRESS

utorontopress.com

LIBRARY AND ARCHIVES CANADA CATALOGUING IN PUBLICATION

Davidov, Veronica, 1978–, author
    Long night at the Vepsian Museum: the forest folk of Northern Russia and the struggle for cultural survival / Veronica Davidov.

(Teacher culture : UTP ethnographies for the classroom)
Includes bibliographical references and index
Issued in print and electronic formats.
ISBN 978-1-4426-3619-4 (hardcover).—ISBN 978-1-4426-3618-7
(softcover).—ISBN 978-1-4426-3620-0 (EPUB).—ISBN 978-1-4426-3621-7 (PDF)

    1. Veps—Russia (Federation)—Sheltozero—History.   2. Veps—Russia (Federation)—Sheltozero—Ethnic identity.   3. Veps—Russia (Federation)—Sheltozero—Social life and customs.   4. Veps—Russia (Federation)—Sheltozero—Religion.   5. Ethnology—Russia (Federation)—Sheltozero.   6. Sheltozero (Russia)—Religious life and customs.
    I. Title. II. Series: Teaching culture

DK34.V4D38 2017   947'150049454   C2017-904214-9
                                                         C2017-904215-7

We welcome comments and suggestions regarding any aspect of our publications—please feel free to contact us at news@utphighereducation.com or visit our Internet site at www.utorontopress.com.

North America	UK, Ireland, and continental Europe
5201 Dufferin Street	NBN International
North York, Ontario, Canada, M3H 5T8	Estover Road, Plymouth, PL6 7PY, UK
	ORDERS PHONE: 44 (0) 1752 202301
2250 Military Road	ORDERS FAX: 44 (0) 1752 202333
Tonawanda, New York, USA, 14150	ORDERS E-MAIL: enquiries@nbninternational.com

ORDERS PHONE: 1–800–565–9523
ORDERS FAX: 1–800–221–9985
ORDERS E-MAIL: utpbooks@utpress.utoronto.ca

Every effort has been made to contact copyright holders; in the event of an error or omission, please notify the publisher.

The University of Toronto Press acknowledges the financial support for its publishing activities of the Government of Canada through the Canada Book Fund.

Printed in the United States of America.

To Fionn

CONTENTS

ILLUSTRATIONS

ACKNOWLEDGMENTS

All cultural production depends on the material conditions that allow it to emerge. When it comes to this book, I am grateful to the Fulbright Scholar Program and to the Maastricht University Faculty of Arts and Social Sciences for funding this research. I am grateful to my Fulbright "hosts"—Professor Pivoev and the Petrozavodsk State University Department of Culturology. I am thankful to Dr. Zinaida Strogalshikova and Dr. Nina Zaytseva at the Institute of Language, Literature, and History of the Karelian Research Centre of the Russian Academy of Sciences for their time, interviews, and willingness to share their experiences and knowledge as both scholars and members of the Vepsian community. I am grateful to Sheltozero, Rybreka, and Vekhruchey villagers for granting my interview requests, housing me, feeding me, and offering me many cups of tea (special thanks in that department go to my landlady), giving me rides, loaning me books, letting me dig through their family photo albums, and in general humouring my being a quintessentially nosy ethnographer. Most importantly, I am so grateful to the staff of the Sheltozero Veps Ethnographic Museum, which was such a warm and welcoming environment; it was through the museum that I was able to meet and engage the key informants in my book—members of the Vepsian Choir, village women dedicated to keeping Vepsian language alive, the women who participated in Museum Night, which forms the basis of the culminating chapter of this book. And I am endlessly grateful to have met Nataliya Ankhimova, the director of the museum; her extraordinary kindness, curiosity, energy, sense of humour, deep love for her culture and community make her one of the most amazing people I have ever had the pleasure to meet in all my anthropological journeys. Without her, this book (and the film I made during my stay in Sheltozero) would simply not exist. I am also grateful to my friends and colleagues who read drafts of this, provided feedback, helped with editing and constructive criticism—in particular Barbara Andersen and Anya Bernstein. I thank my colleague at the

Monmouth University, geographer Geoffrey Fouad, who generously created a map for me to use for this book. I thank John Barker and Anne Brackenbury at the University of Toronto Press for inviting me to tell the story of contemporary Veps in this wonderful ethnographic format, and the anonymous reviewers who provided clear, thoughtful, and extremely helpful feedback. I am, as ever, grateful to my adviser and professors from my graduate school days. I have been applying everything they taught me about thoughtful ethnography and good anthropology to each project I have undertaken since my dissertation, and my scholarship is rooted in the intellectual tools I gained in the New York University anthropology program. And finally, I am so grateful to, and for, my loving family, who have supported my academic endeavours, even though they regularly include my running off to faraway places for long stretches of time.

PREFACE

English-language ethnographies of post-Soviet indigenous groups have histori-cally highlighted "famous" Siberian ethnic groups in the eastern part of Russia. Virtually no ethnographic literature exists about indigenous groups in the northwestern, "European" part of Russia. No ethnographic work has been written about Vepsy (Veps in English)—the indigenous people who are the subjects of my study—by non-Russian academics. Their historical and ethno-graphic realities are overlooked and marginalized in the ever-expanding liter-ature on global indigenous experiences.

Contemporary Veps are a small indigenous group; in the 2002 Russian census they numbered only 8,240. Their language is classified within the western Baltic branch of the Finno-Ugric languages, which includes indigenous groups such as the Vods and Izhors. Linguists classify Vepsian language into three dialect-based groups: Northern Veps, who live in Karelia on the south-western part of Lake Onega and are the focus of this ethnographic work); Sredniye (Middle) Veps, who live in the northeastern part of Leningradskaya Oblast' and the northwestern part of the Vologodskaya Oblast'; and Southern Veps, who live in the Boksitogorskiy Region of Leningradskaya Oblast'. There is also a small diasporic community in Siberia, descended from Veps who migrated there during Stolypin's land reform;[1] they do not maintain ties with the Veps still living on the territories of Karelia, but they were included in a study of Vepsian language practices that was recently jointly conducted by Finnish and Russian researchers.

As a child in the Soviet school system, I learned about Veps, who belonged to a group of ethnic peoples broadly known as **chud'**, meaning "different" or "others." At the time, in Soviet teachings, they, and other related ethnic groups, were represented as one of the many peoples "shedding" their tradi-tions and beliefs, and becoming "proper" Soviet citizens. As an adult anthropol-ogist, educated in the American university system, I searched for ethnographic

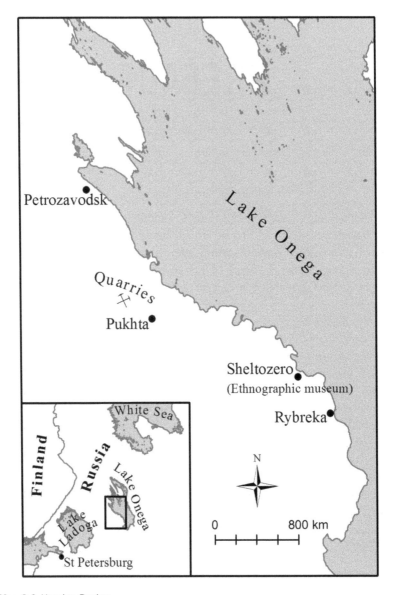

Map 0.1 Vepsian Region

literature about Veps but found nothing, except for a few esoteric texts focused on Vepsian linguistics. So I decided that I would write an ethnography of the Vepsian experience, and in the spring and summer of 2011, I conducted field-work among then, thanks to funding from the Fulbright Scholar Program and the help of the Department of Culturology of Petrozavodsk State University.

This ethnography is based on four months of participant observation in Sheltozero and surrounding villages, namely Rybreka and Vekhruchey; interviews in Sheltozero and Petrozavodsk (including with scholars at the Karelian Academy of Sciences, and Vepsian grassroot linguistic activists); collaborative ethnographic engagement with the workers of the Sheltozero ethnographic museum, during which I produced a documentary called "Museum Night" (focusing on the same event that is the subject of Chapter 5 of this book); and archival research, focused on village histories preserved at the museum and regional publications, including *Kodima* (Native Land), a Vepsian monthly newspaper that was launched in 1993. Logistically, I organized my ethnographic work by establishing a living base in the village, where I rented a room from one of the families whose house was equipped to accept boarders, as they regularly hosted tourists who stayed for multiple days. I also had a sublet room in Petrozavodsk, where I stayed occasionally before or after interviews I conducted in the city, at the university or Academy of Sciences, or at Vepsian community organizations. My Fulbright affiliation helped me tap into the academic network around Vepsian culture and language in the region, and the head of the ethnographic museum, Nataliya Ankhimova, took me "under her wing" and introduced me to anyone I had interest in interviewing, or anyone she thought would be an interesting person for me to talk to in the village. The museum, where I spent much of my time, was a space where I got to know many women of Sheltozero, and to the extent that I was able to establish relationships with men, it was largely through them. Whether I was interested in interviewing miners or World War II veterans, these men were frequently their husbands, or fathers, or grandfathers.

Every history is accompanied by and expressed through the concomitant production of knowledge about the subject of that history. The Veps are no exception. Although in recent years, the politics of cultural and linguistic revival have both inspired and been reinforced by a number of native scholars and public intellectuals, for centuries, Veps have been subjects of accounts and knowledge production located outside of the community. As I discuss in the book, they are cognizant and in some ways reflexive about their role as a "studied" people; in seeing their culture mirrored through the processes of knowledge production by folklorists, ethnographers, and the like, they have come to recognize which aspects of their identity possesses cultural capital "of interest" to scholars. Although this is undoubtedly important to keep in mind when considering issues of representation and self-representation (discussed at length in the final chapter, "The Long Night of Museums"), the point I want to make here is about the entanglement that being a subject of study generates. Although the narratives of small-numbered indigenous peoples of Russia (and indigenous peoples elsewhere) are frequently ones of isolation and continuity of tradition, such narratives are usually historically false. The case of Veps is no exception. As I show throughout the chapters, Veps, especially the Vepsian subgroup that is the subject of this book—Northern Veps, also known as Onega Veps—have had labour, economic, and cultural entanglements with worlds beyond their villages and subsistence territories for centuries. Certainly from the tenth century on, Veps were entangled with Russian culture not only as economic and political actors but also as characters in the narratives that the Russian and then the Soviet state had of themselves: narratives with powerful political implications that generated categories of difference and exclusion, integration policies, entitlements, and forms of marginalization. At no point after the formation of the state and the incorporation of their territories into its domain did Veps, even in the most remote and "traditional" areas, exist apart from or outside of the state.

Part of that aligned and integrated existence has been the gradually emergent understanding that, as a small-numbered indigenous group, they were considered to be repositories of "traditions" and folklore and linguistic diversity. And, in line with that, a part of how Vepsian communities were seen and known by outsiders was a result of scientific expeditions by ethnologists, linguists, folklorists, historians, and the like.

I, as an anthropologist, was not the first (nor will I be the last) "outside" scholar to add my version of Vepsian culture to the body of knowledge already in existence about them, and after this fieldwork and during the process of assembling it into a manuscript, I contemplated what it would mean to be an "expert on Veps" (as I was once introduced to a fellow anthropologist at an American Anthropological Association Meeting). What did it mean for me, after the months I had spent in the village, to be an "expert"? On the one hand, I now have knowledge to share that is not only new to many who have never heard of Veps but also interesting to my ethnographic subjects themselves. As the director of the Sheltozero museum wrote to me recently, after receiving the documentary film I had made about the museum, it was interesting to see how I assembled the different parts of their stories together. On the other hand, am I really an "expert" compared to the multitude of Vepsian scholars who study and document and comment on and analyse their own culture? The issues of expertise and production of knowledge are loaded ones in the epistemic economy, all the more so when the knowledge in question is about indigenous communities that in many places around the world have been spoken for far more than they have been listened to.

In fact, this is in part why I chose—or, in a sense, was compelled—to centre this book, at times loosely, at other times more explicitly, around the museum, even though my own primary interests as a scholar do not lie in museum studies. As an anthropologist grounded in the tradition of holism, I am interested in cultural production, and I envision this book as contributing to indigenous studies and to anthropology in general, because in addition to telling the story of Veps, an indigenous group "understudied" in global scholarship, this work is also an example of a collaborative ethnography made possible by an existent strong praxis of cultural production and curation already present in Sheltozero, thanks to the museum. I still wanted to—and do—tell the story of Vepsian subsistence, their historical relationship with the unique natural resources located on their territories, their disenfranchisement during the transition to post-Soviet governance; but the consistent tethering of all arcs of their story back to the museum is designed to help the reader keep in mind that indigenous communities are not simply objects—or even subjects—of ethnographic work. They are consistently engaged in cultural labour in authoring their stories. In this particular case, the expertise of ethnographic subjects— which can sometimes be diluted or illegible to readers, who are used to locating the expertise in the voice of anthropologist—is explicated thanks to the presence of the museum, which, by the virtue of its existence in an ethnographic site, subverts the traditional dichotomies of indigenous communities serving as "raw" (to invoke Levi-Strauss) cultural data, and ethnographers assembling it into "cooked" expert analyses of cultural phenomena.

I am not trying to reify the concept of the museum as an interrogated marker of cultural authority; museums as institutions have a long entanglement with colonialism and imperialism, and the history of indigenous museums is a far from unambiguous indigenous reclamation of control over one's cultural narrative (see Kreps 1998; Arnoldi 1999). But what is notable is that "indigenous museums," as spaces, have often been centralized and de-territorialized from the communities they represent. The Quai Branly Museum in Paris features indigenous art and artifacts from Africa, Asia, the Americas, and Oceania, much of it from former colonial territories. The Royal Museum for Central Africa in Tervuren, Belgium (dating back to King Leopold II's colonial reign over the Congo Free State) is an ethnographic museum focused on the Congo. Such de-territorializations are not necessarily transnational; the National Museum of Anthropology in Mexico City hosts exhibits about contemporary indigenous cultures in the rural parts of the state. And the Vepsian museum that is the lynchpin of the cultural history and memory of the Vepsian community is an example of a grassroots indigenous ethnographic museum located within the indigenous community whose experience it represents. The Sheltozero ethnographic museum came out of the Soviet practice of promoting local cultural institutions and local cultural workers, in an attempt to create a labour sector out of "culture"—which made it easier to tether the multiplicity of cultural narratives throughout the diverse, multilingual and multicultural USSR to a centralized Marxist-Leninist doctrine and unifying national imaginary. Museumification processes that highlight and celebrate local culture and history even precede the Soviet period in Russia as a tool of governance; as Fein (2013: 146–47) notes, "The objectified knowledge held in regional museums mediated between imperial interests and local agency. Museum workers collected objects of the region's nature and people that were useful to state initiatives like railway-building and peasant resettlement, but in the process of pursuing these approved scientific projects, some began to resent attempts at state control. These many types of local museums, gubernia museums, municipal museums, museums of statistical commissions, and Geographical Society museums would converge in the 1920s into regional-studies museums (*kraevedcheskie muzei*) operating on a reformulated, standardized concept of *region* designed to serve central state planning."

A grassroots or "homegrown" museum today stands as an interesting example for anthropologists working in a global context in which indigeneity as a political category has been a site of power struggles over what is "authentic culture" and, more importantly, who is recognized as an "authenticator." The ability to self-represent through the medium of a museum has been a tool for indigenous communities around the world to pre-empt and respond to the outsider gaze while also using the idea of a museum as a symbolic vernacular of "modernity" and "civilization" on their own terms. In my first book (Davidov 2013), based on my fieldwork in the Ecuadorian Amazon, I described an indigenous village, in a region that has become a popular ecotourism and cultural tourism destination, that was unique in building their own in situ ethnographic museum—the first of its kind—and how its presence created a space for negotiating different dynamics with tourists than the ones more commonly seen in other "destination" villages. Most notably, the museum in that situation allowed for "exotic" items such as poison-tipped arrows and grass skirts to be formally curated as examples of "history" and "tradition," thus minimizing the informal "curation" of everyday life through "tourist realism" that was endemic in other villages, where tourists came in droves in search of "exotic Indians" and radical alterity (Bruner and Kirshenblatt-Gimblett 1994).

But whereas in the Amazon such a "homegrown" museum was *sui generis*, in the post-Soviet context, indigenous communities have, in a sense, inherited existing museum "hardware" put in place during the Soviet period to both service their own communities in mirroring back to them their own experiences and, to some extent, authoring the image of Vepsian culture as presented to outsiders. Ideological and didactic as it was, the Soviet institutionalization of regional studies museums created a built-in positionality for indigenous communities to be formal producers and authors of stories about themselves. And in addition to my specific thematic interests in Vepsian culture and history, largely centred around their relationship with the natural world and the natural resources around them, I saw doing ethnography in a community with an established homegrown ethnographic museum in its midst as an opportunity to contribute to the anthropology of indigeneity and the anthropology of museums methodologically—by explicitly contextualizing my own field research within the field of expertise that predated and superseded my presence in Sheltozero. Anthropologists see themselves (and are seen) as cultural workers, and despite an emphasis since the *Writing Culture* turn on "shared ethnography" and the decolonization of the politics of representation, ethnographic audiences are still primed to regard the anthropological, authorial voice as the expert figure, the one who will interpret the culture under study to them. And while I do not abscond my anthropological responsibility of doing that, I also take the opportunity to tell the stories in this book with an ongoing inclusion of the museum and the museum workers into a shared ethnographic "we."

To return to Veps and their self-constitution in history through becoming subjects of knowledge production: such entanglement with "outsiders" went beyond national borders. In addition to Russian and then Soviet scholars, another group of knowledge producers who have engaged with Vepsian culture and history in significant ways that continue through today are the Finns. As will be discussed in the account of World War II years in Vepsian communities in Chapter 1, Veps have long been subjects of interest within Finnish linguistic and cultural scholarship. In fact, this Finnish preoccupation with Veps as "kin" dramatically affected the nature and ethos of the Finnish occupation of Vepsian territories during World War II. This entanglement with Finland and Finnish knowledge producers plays a large role in shaping cultural and economic ties between Veps and Finns today—but also possibly an even more important one in the Vepsian cultural revival itself. That second role dates back to the nineteenth century, when Finnish scholars became very interested in Veps and in Vepsian language as a "kin" culture and language. In 1842 and 1845, the famous folklorist and scholar of Karelian runes, and the author of the *Kalevala*, Elias Lönnrot came to the region to study Vepsian language; his visit was followed by a research trip by August Alkvist. Their linguistic material, as well as data gathered in the 1880s by Finnish scholars Emile Setyala and Lauri Kettunen, was foundational for Vepsian language studies. In general, the uniqueness of the Vepsian language was perceived by Finnish scholars to be a testament to its "archaic" nature, which they considered to be important for studying the early stages of the Finnish language. This approach was typical of nineteenth-century European social sciences, which perceived certain ethnic and linguistic groups as existing in a different temporality, at an earlier stage of cultural development, and thus able to serve as mirrors of windows to more "evolved" cultures' own past and heritage. The fact that Finnish studies of Vepsian were foundational for the corpus of Vepsian linguistics in general, and the fact that they arose out of this research agenda, shaped for many years to come the notion that Vepsian language was static and "arrested" at a particular stage of development—a perspective summed up by Kettunen's oft-quoted statement that Vepsian is the "Sanskrit" of Baltic-Finnish languages. This interest in Veps as an "archaic" peoples was not limited to linguistics; their cultural practices (especially among Southern Veps) were considered by Finnish ethnographers to be instances of *zhivaya starina* (living antiquity) for over a hundred years.

Historically, Finnish scholars primarily focused on Vepsian language, while Russian ethnographers focused on Vepsian culture. Today, of course, as we will see in the book, homegrown Vepsian intellectuals spearhead the study of both and have successfully fused scholarship with cultural revival and cultural survival activism. But the early body of scholarship about Veps consistently represented them as an "ancient" people at the "sunset" of their culture—because of the process of *obrusenie*, Russianization. As Vepsian scholar Kolmogorov wrote, "Not in the distant lands, but close to the capital, an entire ethnicity is living out its last days, because the inevitable process of assimilation with the Russian nation will force the Kaivan streams to merge with the 'Russian sea' and disappear in it" (cited in Zaytseva n.d.).

All this history—as it was being enacted and recorded—is the crucible in which the Vepsian identity as an indigenous people, as an ethno-political category in Russia, was forged. It warrants noting that this two-pronged focus on language and culture accommodated Vepsian environment and human-nature relationships in Vepsian communities in a very limited way, primarily through the lens of cosmology and forest folklore. I mention this because, although this is not explicitly an environmental ethnography, I am an environmental anthropologist. I did my graduate fieldwork, as previously mentioned, in one of the most well-known spaces of nature on earth: the Amazon rainforest. While, of course, all cultures both shape and are shaped by the spaces and constructs of nature and environment that they inhabit physically and symbolically, I was drawn to Veps as ethnographic subjects because their livelihoods were shaped so profoundly, and in a way so hyper-articulated by them in their own self-understanding, by twin forces grounded in their land, their environment. Those two forces are first of all their central position in the long history of extraction of a rare, elite mineral—raspberry quartzite, found only on Vepsian territory, and nowhere else in the world—and second by the cultivation of Karelia as an ecologically "pure" health resort destination by the Russian, then the Soviet state.

Notes

1. The Stolypin Agrarian Reform or Stolypin Land Reform was a series of actions in the area of agricultural administration implemented between 1905 and 1917 by the imperial government, designed to improve peasants' land-tenure conditions through enabling them to obtain land titles and consolidate land plots. The name comes from Pyotr Stolypin, who was the chair of the Council of Ministers of the Russian Empire at this time, and introduced the measures that constituted the reform.

INTRODUCTION

This book, the product of ethnographic fieldwork, and additional archival and historical research, takes the readers to the village of Sheltozero in the Republic of Karelia, on the southwestern side of Lake Onega, a community populated by approximately a thousand people, most of them Vepsy, a numerically small indigenous Finno-Ugric people colloquially known in Russia as "forest folk" for their ascribed intense closeness and affiliation with forests on their ancestral territories. The village straddles two sides of a small river, which rises during springtime when the snow melts, half-flooding the low-lying wooden fishing shacks along the river basin. Indeed, most of the village is made up of traditional wooden houses, although there is a small complex of "modern" apartments, housing predominantly older people whose children have moved out of the village and who have a hard time maintaining their farmhouses in the winter, and the handful of migrants from Armenia and Tajikistan who have moved into the village over the last decade. There are also new, barrack-like constructions—housing for schoolteachers. There are three little grocery stores concentrated near the main road, and a public cafeteria down the road from the sole bus stop in town. Buses pass once, sometimes twice an hour, heading to or from Petrozavodsk, the republic's capital, two hours north. Almost as frequently, one can see passing trucks, carrying giant slabs of black rock—gabbro-diabase, a rare and valuable mineral mined in the quarries near the village, where many of the Sheltozero men work.

The first building a visitor sees when entering the village is the Sheltozero Vepsian Ethnographic Museum. The museum is a sturdy large *izba*[1]—a traditional log house, commemorating the regional history of the Veps. It came from the efforts of Vepsian native folklorist and ethnographer, Ryurik Lonin, who founded the museum in the 1960s and is venerated in the village and the museum as a key figure in the contemporary cultural revival programs spearheaded by Vepsian intellectual elites. Today the museum is one of the

1

Figure 0.1 A road sign marking the entrance to Sheltozero

branches of the National Museum of the Republic of Karelia and is thus a part of cultural preservation and heritage networks on the level of the republic. In the Russian museum nomenclature it is known as a "living history museum," because it is situated in the very community whose experience it represents.

The museum marks the entry into the village—and into this book, as the museum space holds the different topics explored in the book. This is not an artificially manufactured concept; as will become clear, the museum, in its many historical and contemporary functions, both mirrors and represents Vepsian experience and serves as a space where Sheltozero Veps are able to consciously engage with their own past and present through a variety of cultural practices.

ENTERING THE MUSEUM

In front of the museum is a carved wooden statue—**Khozyain** Lesa—the Master of the Forest, the central figure in the traditional cosmology of the Veps. The downstairs rooms feature a reproduction of a traditional Vepsian home, with selected objects and space arrangements full of symbolism and evocative of rituals—a point made clear to groups of local Vepsian schoolchildren, who regularly visit the museum on field trips and have the space interpreted for them through excursions and interactive educational games. The second-floor rooms are exhibition halls that show Vepsian subsistence practices, from farming to mining. There is an exhibit hall devoted to fishing and hunting; a diorama mounted on the wall devoted to **othodnichestvo** (a feudal-era term meaning temporary labour migration, including for the purposes of agriculture, construction, and furnace work); and a historical overview of a nineteenth-century stoneworker brigade. The exhibition text speaks of the glory bestowed on Vepsian stoneworkers, reading as follows: "The extraction and processing of raspberry quartzite demanded skills and knowledge that were passed from generation to generation over the course of centuries. Thus arose entire dynasties of stonemasters."

THE MUSEUM'S HISTORY OF ITSELF AND ITS FOUNDER

The room up one flight of stairs is filled with glass cases and wall mounts that document the cultural history of Vepsian identity politics. Here, one will find homage to the aforementioned local ethnographer, Ryurik Lonin, who lived a long life in Sheltozero, and whose spectre, in a sense, animates many aspects of cultural life of the village and, consequently, many pages of this book. Ironically, this icon in the Vepsian cultural preservation movement actually has a classically Russian name: Ryurik is the name of a famous Russian Prince from Novgorod. But how Lonin came by that name—his stoneworker father brought it back with him after his stints as a seasonal labour migrant to that region—is actually an example of the cultural mélange typical of the Vepsian communities at the centre of this ethnography; their long-standing free (to an extent) movement as stoneworkers, somewhat unique during the feudal period history of labour migration, will be discussed further on. Lonin was born in 1930 in the Vepsian village of Kaskisruchey, about 10 kilometres from Sheltozero, and lived through the Finnish occupation of the region during World War II as a schoolboy (as will be discussed in Chapter 1). He completed school through 7th grade and subsequently received vocational education in the locksmith trade, which was his first profession; eventually he became an electric welder and worked in the **sovkhoz** workshop.

As a locksmith, he sometimes travelled to various villages around the region, visiting people's homes. He became interested in historical objects after finding an antique anvil in the basement of the house he bought with his wife shortly after they were married (author's interview with Anna Lonina, 2011). This fuelled his growing interest in collecting Vepsian household objects, which—with desirable new technologies (like the latest sewing machine model) arriving in Vepsian households—were relegated to the status of "junk" before Lonin consolidated them and gave them a new cultural life as museum artifacts. According to interviews I conducted, before he became a venerated hero of Vepsian cultural preservation, Lonin was initially perceived as a somewhat of a Quixotic figure. His widow, whom I interviewed during my fieldwork, recounted her frustrations with her spouse early in their married life, when Grandfather, as she called him, filled their house from floor to ceiling: "He would beg or buy these things off, and in those villages, they had more things left over than we do here. We had the municipal centre here, and in other villages, they used those old objects more, so washbasins were copper, tables and chairs were handmade, so were all the wardrobes."

Later, she recounted, after he was allotted the first dedicated space for the museum (two rooms in the library, before the establishment of the museum in its current incarnation), "Everything, even our photos, he took to the museum. I turn around and something else was gone."

Today Lonin is a revered figure within the village, and this is evident in the museum. Among the artifacts representing Vepsian material culture there are displays dedicated to the material culture of Lonin himself: his photographs, from childhood through old age; notebooks; correspondence; his hat and horn-rimmed glasses (and their case); his leather briefcase with metal clasps; and the large stamp he used on official museum correspondence.

In the adjoining shelves commemorating the life and works of Lonin, visitors can see archives and documents of the Soviet state's uneven policies toward the Veps—oscillating between support for cultural continuity and revival on the one hand and assimilation coupled with linguistic repression on the other—as well as bookshelves of rare and out-of-print books written by Soviet and Russian scholars about Veps.

Then follows a room dedicated to the Veps National **Volost'** (an autonomous municipality) that existed for a brief stretch of only 10 years. The displays in this room contain photographs and biographies of Vepsian intellectual

Figure 0.2 A shelf at the museum dedicated to Lonin's personal relics

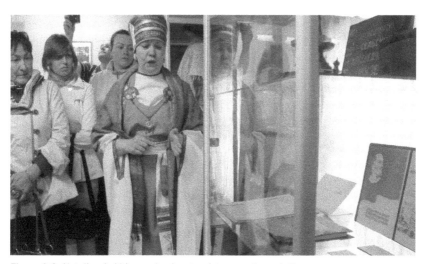

Figure 0.3 Nataliya Ankhimova leads a tourist group through the museum

elites and activists who spearheaded the foundation of the Volost' in 1994 and protested its subsequent forced dissolution in 2004.

The second floor also houses a central room, where the Sheltozero-based Vepsian Choir, in existence since 1936, performs for visitors from far away. The importance of song and singing to Veps cannot be overstated, as music is one of their most distinctive cultural outputs. The choir, founded by Karelian National Artist Vasiliy Kononov, has been an important institution of cultural preservation and, to some extent, cultural reconstruction. In addition to new adaptations of old songs, the choir has created new variations and choreographic interpretations of folk material. The choir is all ages (a separate children's choir was in existence for a while but has been discontinued due to financial insolvency). It tours extensively both in Russia and abroad and has performed and won awards (a point of pride for the participants I interviewed) at festivals in Norway, Finland, Sweden, Hungary, Poland, and Estonia. The choir is also one of the main organizers of the major Vepsian cultural festival, Tree of Life, that for the past 25 years has taken place in Vinnitsi, a Vepsian village in the Leningradskaya Oblast',[2] and draws Veps from the different ethno-geographical "branches."

Today the choir is led by choirmaster and accompanist Sergei Ul'bakov, a Sheltozero native, who told me proudly in an interview that the choir plays an important role in the preservation of ancient songs, practices, traditions, rituals, and dances. When the chorus performs for tourists, they incorporate traditional music-making objects into their music, such as rocks gathered on the shores of Lake Onega (the site, incidentally, of the interview).

The women in the choir "interpret" classic themes in Vepsian songs, high-lighting their sometimes lyrical, sometimes ribald meaning, and building humorous rapport with the audience around familiar gender tropes, as, for instance, in a song about a rooster in trouble with his hen paramour. The choir performs in traditional clothing: women come out in sarafan (pinafore) dresses that are fashioned out of silk, usually in earthy tones (brown, olive green, dark beige). The dresses are worn over festively embroidered shirts, elaborate embroidery being a part of Vepsian costumes for special occasions, with designs varying depending on the ages and life stages of the women.[3] The women wear *kokoshniks*, traditional tiara-like headdresses that are paired with sarafans. The men's costumes are white shirts over dark linen pants, with a rope-like belt, decorated in the same colors as the embroidery: predominantly red and gold, with some green sprinkled in here and there.

On days when tourist groups aren't visiting the museum, the local Vepsian schoolchildren gather for educational programs, and the village elders come for cultural preservation activities, such as the "Vepsian language teas." Vepsian language today is a case study in linguistic revival. As Laura Siragusa, a linguistic anthropologist who studied Vepsian linguistic activism, wrote, "Literacy became an emblem of political action as a way to promote the Vepsian language within a multi-ethnic society such as that of the Republic of Karelia." Siragusa notes that some of the late–Soviet era Vepsian cultural preservation initiatives, requesting governmental support to promote village life and reverse migration to urban centres, were in fact actually designed in the service of maintaining and preserving

Figure 0.4 The Vepsian Choir performs for tourists

the Vepsian language (Siragusa 2012: 22). Such "language teas" are likely an example of what Vepsian intellectual elites had in mind as place-based activities that leveraged a local Vepsian-speaking population as a cultural resource.

For most of its history, Vepsian has been an oral language, and this has created a precedent, in a sense, of its written incarnation being synonymous with academic or educational contexts, on both macro-scales (dictionaries being assembled, longitudinal linguistic studies being conducted) and micro-scales (cultural workers in museums and Vepsian cultural centres assembling and cataloguing archaic words and turns of phrases that emerge from organic conversations, much like sharing recipes). Vepsian linguist Nina Zaytseva, who has made the promotion and preservation of "Living Vepsian Speech" (as she calls it) her life's project, noted:

> Vepsian language, for most of its history, was spoken language, so it did not develop in the same way as written languages do. Living Vepsian speech was recorded on tapes thousands of times during many ethnolinguistic expeditions, and all of its multi-century wealth is diligently fixed and carefully preserved. But Vepsian language as such does not reflect many realities of contemporary world—we need new words. And we are very cautious about introducing new words into standard speech: there is a special terminological committee, which carefully studies the necessity of this or that word at this moment in time and "constructs" it based on word-formation models that characterize Vepsian language. We do not have the goal of enriching Vepsian vocabulary with, for instance, scientific terminology, but words that reflect the realities of modern life are necessary for everyday communication, including for teaching children and youth the language.... In Petrozavodsk there is a successful conversational club "Vepsian Conversations." So people of the older generation who come to the meetings, at first they don't understand everything about how the youth talk, but then they acknowledge—yes, that is exactly right, that's how it should be spoken.[4]

Linguistic "updating" initiatives of this kind keep Vepsian language "alive" and come into being primarily in the urban context of Petrozavodsk, where they are centred around the linguistics department of Petrozavodsk State University, a kind of hub for Vepsian linguists and language activists. Equally important, however, is the task of the Sheltozero museum in clarifying and recording archaic uses of the language. The ever-expanding comprehensive written record of the spoken language has value in and of itself in terms of cultural and linguistic preservation, but it also functions as a kind of linguistic DNA database for the language revival project.

Formal events shift seamlessly into informal get-togethers in the museum's space, in particular in the communal area that hosts community events.

Vepsian language teas morph into hang-outs, and the museum slips back and forth between being a formal space for specific, codified events and serving as an informal space where local politics are discussed, and hopes and complaints are articulated. In addition, the museum is a local archive, holding historical materials and out-of-print books on various aspects of Vepsian history: from an anthology of Vepsian fairy tales to a compendium of (often terrifying) mining lore from the 1930s and 1940s and Soviet-era ethnologies of Karelian ethno-linguistic minorities, including the Veps.

A tour of the museum is also an easy way to introduce the cast of human and non-human characters and artifacts that populates this book: the Forest Master; the brigades of miners; samples of the rare minerals that come from Vepsian lands; traditional tools of the Vepsian hunters; mementos of the Finnish occupation during World War II; photographs of the Vepsian National Choir's national and international performances; a collage showing photos of the Vepsian activists instrumental to the foundation of the Vepsian National Volost'; and the blue, green, and yellow flag that represents forest, lake, and sun and commemorates the brief existence of the Volost'. The museum tells the history of Veps, and in this book I endeavour to do the same. The chapters offer an ethnographic insight into their traditional beliefs, newly contested subsistence practices, formative historical moments, and contemporary political struggles, while at the same time showing how Veps make meaning of their history and their unfolding future through and around the central space of the ethnographic museum, which serves a number of curatorial, social, and political purposes in the village. Each chapter opens with a museum vignette that leads into the topic of the chapter, providing an overview of the relevant themes for understanding Vepsian experience, and also showing how the Sheltozero Veps incorporate those experiences into their village history and their personal narratives.

The first chapter offers a historical and cultural overview of the Vepsian position in Russia as a small-numbered indigenous minority belonging to the Finno-Ugric minority group. It will familiarize the readers with Vepsian cultural and political history and offer a more in-depth introduction to the linguistic and cultural subgroup of the Northern Veps, who are the subject of this work. The chapter starts with a review of the historical arc of Vepsian identity politics and their long-standing complex engagement with the Russian and Soviet states. Primarily focusing on the period between the eighteenth century—when Tsar Peter I developed an ironworks and weapon-making industry in the region and factory work started supplementing agriculture as a primary occupation for Veps—through today, this chapter reviews the subsistence practices and the political economy of Vepsian livelihoods, including hunting, gathering, farming, mining and stoneworking, logging and woodworking, pottery, and barge hauling. These practices are contextualized by significant historical junctures at which the Vepsian livelihoods were transformed in various ways, most notably by the Soviet revolution, which changed the nature of village life and subsistence organization through collectivization and the reorganization of traditional farm holdings into kolkhozes and sovkhozes (the two types of collective farms). The chapter then traces the more recent history of Veps, from World War II and the Finnish occupation of the region through the "liquidation of villages without prospects" and the subsequent resettlement of Veps in the 1960s—the decade when Vepsian cultural revitalization began and Veps started the shift from being "the forest folk" to being indigenous minorities in a Soviet state. The latter part of the chapter traces the various campaigns of cultural and linguistic revival that Veps have undertaken since the 1960s, including efforts by urban Vepsian intellectual elites to promote a unified Vepsian language, and concludes by profiling a 10-year period during which the Veps attempted to leverage cultural and linguistic revival initiatives to seek political sovereignty. This was at a moment when post-Soviet politics were being reconfigured, following Boris Yeltsin's famous quip to the regions in 1990: "*Berite suvereniteta, skol'ko proglotite!*" (Take as much sovereignty as you can swallow!) Although the famous "parade of sovereignties" that followed is usually remembered as the progressive declaration of sovereignty by former Soviet republics in 1991, the ethos of that policy encouraged smaller sovereignty initiatives as well, including increased autonomy of other, smaller, political units. In that political climate, Veps lobbied for and organized the creation of the Veps National Volost', seeking to have a place in the hierarchy of the political and economic "Masters" who shape the fate of the village. I chronicle the inception and the ending of the Volost'—a politically autonomous regional body that lasted exactly 10 years—drawing on interviews with village and Petrozavodsk activists involved in the politics of the creation of the Volost' as well as on the assessments of the Volost' and its demise by Sheltozero residents.

While the pre-state, tsarist, and early Soviet history of Veps is recapitulated from historical materials and secondary sources, the elder generation in Vepsian villages remember first-hand the period of World War II, the Finnish occupation, and the period of collectivization; historical material is therefore integrated with material from life history interviews in the latter part of the chapter.

The second chapter focuses on the cosmological universe of the Veps: a syncretic system of beliefs that since the tenth century has incorporated Russian Orthodox Christianity while maintaining a strong canon of nature spirits. The chapter starts with an overview of the Vepsian beliefs in forest spirits—**Khozyayeva** (Masters)—and their role as regulatory forces of balance, symmetrical exchange, and "propriety" within the forest and between villagers. This section of the chapter focuses specifically on the aspect of this cosmology that involves written contracts historically entered into between cowherders and the Forest Masters, analysing the different elements of this contractual practice and the assumptions that underlie it with regard to mediated forms of obligation and responsibility in local-scale human-nature relationships. The chapter then offers an analysis of how the Veps' general contractual relationships with the Forest Masters have always been connected to, and mirrored, other social, economic, and political contracts, such as the ones negotiated with the state. I tie the contractual nature of the relationship between the Veps and the Forest Masters to the practices and expectations that underlie the regulatory framework, engaging dynamics and domains that go beyond the village and form a moral economy that moves fluidly between scales (village, region, state) and across domains (spiritual, political, commercial), and analysing how such a regulatory framework around exchange, balance, and fairness encompasses social contracts between Veps and the different incarnations of the state.

The third chapter delves into an important part of the Vepsian story: the history of their homeland as a resource environment, mobilized as such by the Russian then the Soviet state. A popular Soviet-era song went, "Long will you dream of Karelia ... the eyelashes of the spruce trees over the blue eyes of the lakes." The first section of the chapter describes how the Vepsian part of Karelia was historically cultivated as a nature and health tourism destination; the designation of Karelian lakesides as elite vacation zones dates back to Peter the Great's establishment of Russia's first "healing resort" in the region. Then I describe the parallel rise of the mining industry in the region, developed around "elite" mineral resources of the Northern Veps: the luxurious raspberry quartzite, known in common parlance as "the tsar's stone," quite cosmopolitan in its circulation and used exclusively for prestigious objects and landmarks, from Napoleon's sarcophagus to Lenin's mausoleum and the Moscow metro; the sturdy gabbro-diabase, used for Soviet infrastructure projects; and the "premium," highly valued Karelian wood. I discuss how, for over a century, the Veps experienced nature tourism, logging, and mining as media of desirable and beneficial contracts with the state: contracts that mirrored their cultural values around their natural environment, as reflected in their cosmological contracts with the Forest Masters.

The fourth chapter centres on the present-day anxieties experienced by the Veps of Sheltozero around the twofold privatization of their lakeshores and forests. *Chastniki* (private actors) are buying up the portions of the lakeshore in order to develop luxurious nature tourism resorts, cutting off Vepsian access to their lakes without any inclusion or compensation. As well, following the implementation of the new Russian Forest Code in 2008, all Russian forests and resources contained therein have become privatized. I show how the mining and logging companies that have taken over the deregulated, formerly state-managed logging and mining industries in the region figure as new, "bad masters" in Vepsian perceptions, supplanting and displacing the spirit Masters themselves through the destruction of their physical habitat. In this chapter, I introduce two concepts that were repeatedly invoked for me by my interlocutors: **za granitsu,** an imaginary of a non-specific space "abroad" or "beyond borders," that signifies Vepsian estrangement and alienation from the natural resources that originate in their land but are exported without creating generative social relations; and **bezpredel,** a word that means "without boundaries" and is used to condemn the accelerated and exploitative regime of resource extraction associated with the privatization of the regional industries.

The final chapter provides a coda to the book, showing, through an ethnographic snapshot of 24 hours, how Vepsian villagers, in particular women, integrate memories of the past and anxieties and hopes about the future. The Vepsian Ethnographic Museum, following recent international practices, organizes a "Museum Night" for the villagers, where the museum reopens after hours for specially curated educational activities, including a *viktorina*—a game where teams of Sheltozero women, most of them members of the Vepsian Choir, compete to correctly answer questions about Vepsian culture and traditions. The viktorina is structured in a way that organically encourages collective reflections on Vepsian past and present. The prize for the game is an excursion for all participants through Vepsian lands the very next day, chauffeured by the village school bus driver. Visiting important local places—stretches of the forest, old churches, and lakeshores—the women reflect upon and relate to the familiar yet transforming geographies and landscapes around them.

Taken together, the chapters coalesce into an ethnography that links the past and the present of a people who have been understudied outside of regional Russian and Finnish academia. In that, this book contributes to the global body of knowledge about indigenous communities, which is skewed toward knowledge production about indigenous communities located outside of Europe and the West. But even beyond that, this book offers an ethnographic and ethnohistorical portrait of a people who, from my perspective as an anthropologist who has worked on topics related to indigenous issues worldwide, offer through their history and positionality a case study that helps us challenge some of the most common tropes about indigeneity, within both public imagination and academic debates. In a pervasive discourse of indigeneity that tethers indigenous identity, indigenous rights, and efforts at cultural revival and survival to a particular (and quite limited) relationship with nature—one that generally pivots around ideas of nature integrity and "preservation," and opposes extractive activities—an indigenous community whose sense of self and cultural pride is inexorably entwined with mining constructively challenges the all-too-frequent naturalization of indigeneity as some kind of magical state of existing in harmony with nature, with opposition to extractive industries becoming some kind of litmus test for "real" indigeneity.

Notes

1. *Krestyanskaya* izba (peasant log cabin) in Russian; the traditional wooden house in Vepsian (and Russian) villages.

2. In 2014, Tree of Life was actually tethered to an academic conference entitled "Veps: History and Modernity."

3. Shirts for daily wear were as a rule not embroidered, or only very plainly embroidered. Festivals, in contrast, were a time for women to show off their embroidered designs; in fact, Onega Vepsian women historically wore two shirts, one on top of another, so that the embroidered edges at the bottom of the shirt would be imbricated in layers, forming a wide embroidered band.

4. Interview conducted in May 2011.

CHAPTER 1

HISTORY AND MEMORY

Like a nesting doll, Vepsian history is enveloped—or, alternately, revealed—in layers. Ensconced in the landscape of Karelia, the ancestral land of Veps, lies Sheltozero—their erstwhile political and past and present cultural locus. The village houses a museum, which, in turn, houses a room that is referred to as "the permanent installation," where Vepsian history is displayed through images, words, and material objects: a map of the lake, carved out of bone and hung on the wall; a piece of cloth, embroidered with red thread—much like the one featured on the cover of this book—and situated under glass in a display case. Whatever the most current exhibit is, visitors to the museum are expected to tether themselves to the historical linearity that is imposed on the non-linear log cabin space of the cosy wooden building by the tour guides, who start at the very beginning of their history. And much like the museum's visitors and guides, we ought to start with the *longue durée* of Vepsian history, which is presented below, drawn from a number of sources. In terms of secondary sources, the most helpful texts to me in this endeavour were the works by contemporary Vepsian scholar Irina Vinokurova, based at the Karelian branch of the Russian Academy of Sciences, and works by another prominent Vepsian scholar (and activist, mentioned throughout the book and also based at the Academy), Zinaida Strogalshikova, including her edited volume based on the conference "Veps—An Indigenous Small-numbered People of Russian Federation: Perspectives of Preservation and Development" that took place in Petrozavodsk in April of 2008. In terms of primary sources, the historical data I assembled into the narrative below was drawn from personal interviews with Strogalshikova and her colleague, Vepsian linguist Nina Zaytseva; the documentation accompanying the permanent exhibit at the museum; and interviews with Sheltozero residents and library staff. I also read and studied autobiographical books by Ryurik Lonin (2004a, 2004b), and consider them to be ethnohistorical primary sources.

For over a thousand years, the southeastern region of what is currently Leningradskaya Oblast' and the southern part of Karelia has been populated by a Baltic-Ugric people called, in the archival sources of that time, Ves'. Their ethnogenesis has been a contested topic in Russian history and anthropology, but historically their fate has been tied with the Slavic expansion north around 1000 AD. As Slavyane (Slavs) colonized the waterways local to the region, mobilizing the lakes and rivers connecting these territories for their trade and expansion purposes, ancient Veps experienced the first instance of assimilation and forced migration, as new Slavic communities resulted in Vepsian populations being relocated to Mezhozerye (the land between Lake Ladoga, Lake Onega, and Lake Beloye) and beyond. Within Russian academia and historiography, Veps were first featured in 1816 in historian N.M. Karamzin's famous 12-volume treatise, *History of the Russian State*. In it, Karamzin argued for a total assimilation and transformation of Veps, along with Meri and Muromi (two other Finno-Ugric tribes), into Slavs, claiming that they had already adopted Slavic traditions, language, and faith. His theory of full assimilation was reproduced in academic works on the Veps uncritically until the 1940s, when works by D.V. Bubrikh and V.V. Pimenov on the ethnogenesis and early history of the Veps complicated the picture, reconceptualizing Veps as a group that had remained culturally and linguistically distinct.

In reality, of course, as is the case with many indigenous groups around the world, and to paraphrase Mark Twain's quip in the *New York Journal* about his own death, rumours of their assimilation were greatly exaggerated. But we should bear in mind that assimilation is a flat metric, one that overlooks the rich cultural syncretism that arises in the context of border cultures and the incorporation of indigenous groups into nation-states, as occurred among the Veps, first within the context of tsarist Russia and then within the context of the Soviet state. This chapter provides a "big picture" overview of the Veps as a linguistic and ethnic community that has been transformed over and over by historical circumstances, continuously negotiating tradition and change in their narrative and understanding of themselves as a people.

VEPSIAN SUBSISTENCE PRACTICES

To understand the legacy and the transformation of a community, it is important to understand their social order and system of organization, which, in the case of indigenous groups, generally predate the social order that comes with its members being subjects of the state and in many cases continue to exist in parallel with the state. For a long time, Vepsian peasant life was largely dictated by their community, called *sber*. The community was a central organizational node that gave shape to life trajectories and handled land distribution and redistribution, collective works, employment, and, prior to the introduction of the mandatory draft in 1847, military recruitment. Communities collectively owned forests, grasslands, and fishing grounds. Various figures of authority, such as elders, deacons, and tax collectors, were elected at community meetings, and disputes between peasants were handled there. Communities were also in charge of fundraising for collective help to people who had fallen on hard times. Historically, communities also elected their own priests, although as the Church became more influential, priests started being appointed by the diocese. Each community had its own pogost, with a church and a cemetery.

Well into the 1930s, Veps lived in large three-or-four-generation households formed through a patrilocal kinship structure, with post-marital residence being established in the house of the husband. In terms of gendered division of labour, historically the head of the family and the household was the eldest patriarch—father or grandfather—the *ižand*, or Master. His wife—the *emag*, or Mistress—managed cattle (in addition to horses), prepared food, wove, and sewed clothes. Men's and women's roles were fairly equal. A widow was entitled to the return of her dowry, while a childless widow was entitled to a living pension, reflecting the years of her work in her husband's household. Historically, Vepsian peasants were agriculturalists. They grew barley, rye, oats, wheat flax, and hops. Livestock—cows, horses, and sheep—played a secondary but important role in Vepsian household production. The herds were necessarily restricted in numbers because of a limited supply of fodder.

Like many other Russian groups with land-based subsistence lifestyles, Veps practiced slash-and-burn agriculture, which they considered to be the most effective method for growing grain crops. As their traditional territories lay in heavily forested areas, Veps implemented one of the oldest methods in the region for preparing forest clearings in the region: they debarked trees up to human height and allowed the trees to dry for a year. In the following spring, such debarked trees would be cut down and left to dry further. Then spaces would be cleared, either for plowing (generally dry areas), or for cultivated meadows (damper patches of land). As the last part of this multi-year process, the downed trees, now completely dried out, would be burned the following year. This produced a layer of topsoil saturated with ash, an effective fertilizer, and took care of the weeds. At that point, a three-year cycle of growing seasons was initiated. The cycle went as follows: turnip was the crop in the first year, followed in the second year by barley and rye, and in the third and final year by oats. The soil at that point became depleted, and the clearing was abandoned or left for horticultural plots. Then a new plot would be cultivated. The state, frowning on this form of land use, sought to limit it as early as 1889, but in northern regions, slash-and-burn agriculture continued to be practiced until the 1930s.

In addition to agriculture, for Veps who lived on lakeshores and rivers, fishing was a major form of subsistence. This is particularly true of the Onega Veps, whose story is told in the pages ahead. Unlike other Veps subgroups, who fished primarily for subsistence, Onega Veps traditionally supplemented their incomes with commercial fishing. Lake Onega was a fertile ground for such an enterprise, rich in over 40 species of fish, including whitefish, lake char, salmon, trout, walleye, pike, grayling, bass, bream, and burbot. The Onega Veps were experienced fishermen, who brought fish to sell to St. Petersburg and Petrozavodsk. Far from a solo enterprise, fishing was a well-organized and communal endeavour; fish for commercial use were caught on big boats used and shared by kindred communities (although some villages practiced fishing restrictively, rather than cooperating with other villages). In addition, each household had its own boats, generally used for subsistence fishing.

"Modernity" is a contingent and often misleading concept, but the modern history of Veps can be said to start with Peter the Great, the tsar of Russia from 1682 until 1725. Peter the Great is known for a series of imperial expansions and reforms, and the development of Russian industry. Against this backdrop, and as a part of his series of reforms, Veps, as a group, became actively incorporated into the structure of the Russian state. Peter the Great's reign also marked the moment when the foundation was laid for the administrative divisions of Vepsian territories that have continued in one form or another until this day.

Figure 1.1 Display of traditional Vepsian fishing practices at the museum

During Peter the Great's reign, the peasants of the Olonets Governorate,[1] which encompassed the territories under discussion in our ethnography, had the status of "national" peasants, that is, peasants who belonged to the state—a new class of serfs, with broader rights than those tethered to a single landlord— but they were still obligated to pay taxes to the state and to meet public work quotas (for instance, participating in road construction and forestry). Veps of that governorate also fell under the classification of state peasants (while the Veps of the adjacent Novgorod Governorate belonged to private landowners, which was the traditional, more restrictive model of serfdom). During the eighteenth century, as a part of his wide-sweeping economic reforms, Peter I started developing military and shipbuilding industries in the Olonets Governorate— the industries that would later ensure Russia's victory in the Great Northern War, fought between 1700 and 1721 between Russia and Sweden, and guarantee Russian access to the Baltic Sea.

In 1703, construction of ironworks and a weapons plant began on the shore of Lake Onega, on Vepsian territories, and it was this industrial hub that gave rise to the city of Petrozavodsk, named Petrine Sloboda[2] at the time, and the contemporary capital of the Republic of Karelia. In order to provide the labour force for booming industries, "state peasants" from the Olonets Governorate were assigned to metallurgical, ironworks, and weapons plants, as well as shipyards. Labour quotas took the place of taxation and the previously discussed public works, and the conscripted workers were even paid a small compensation; as has been the case in many places around the world, the advent of industry was also the inception of some form of wage labour and a cash economy for indigenous communities. Onega Veps were assigned primarily to the plants, although some were deployed for shipbuilding.

Such semi-wage labour—a departure from traditional subsistence agriculture and fishing—integrated Veps into the economic and political networks of the region. That labour history is part of the historical differences in cultural development between Onega Veps and Novgorod Veps; the latter remained more involuted, as their lifestyle was contained within the estate lands of their feudal owners—the reason for later Soviet historians to characterize feudal Veps as retaining a more "archaic" culture for longer.

Labour skills that the Onega Veps learned during their tenure at plants and at shipbuilding yards, in particular carpentry, ended up being transferable once they returned to their villages. This knowledge and skills capital subsequently affected socio-economic development in the region.

It is important to point out that the Onega Veps' centuries-long entanglement in these webs of labour and industry are key and instrumental to the story at the core of this book—the story of an indigenous people who depart from a common and predictable script that expects indigeneity to be aligned with "natural" living (i.e., foraging and or horticulture) or, at the very least, long-standing subsistence-based, rather than market-based, agricultural practices. The Veps of this book are miners and stoneworkers and loggers, and the formation of that cultural identity, although subject to many factors and historical forces, can be traced back to this juncture: the moment at which they, unlike their counterparts in the neighbouring governorate, were designated as state peasants and involved in state-building industrial projects.

This administrative division was reinforced over the course of the following century, and in the new post-revolution Soviet state, the territory of Veps remained administratively divided. In 1924, the greater part of Vepsian Prionezhye (Lake Onega Region), which at that time housed a quarter of the entire Vepsian population, became incorporated into the Karelian Autonomous Social Socialist Republic (KASSR). The rest of the territory became a part of the Leningradskaya Oblast'.[3]

These administrative divisions, as well as the incorporation of a large fraction of the Veps into the urban and industrial labour sectors, meant that at the moment of the formation of the Soviet Union, in 1917, like many other indigenous groups, Veps were seen as a "disappearing" people. But what that perception reflected was the resettlements and labour migrations of Veps beyond the traditional *sber*—not their demographic decline. The first census ever conducted that featured Veps numbered them at 26,700 (according to the first census of the Russian empire, 1897), and the Veps were at their demographic apex in 1926, when they numbered 32,800. This population growth contradicted the speculation of Russian and early Soviet ethnologists who, throughout the nineteenth century and until the 1920s, described Veps as a disappearing people; S.A. Makaryev, the first professional Vepsian ethnographer, who published over 70 works about his people before perishing in Stalin's purges of 1937, countered this notion emphatically.

VEPS IN THE SOVIET ERA

In 1917, following a series of revolutions, the autocratic tsarist state gave way to the new Russian Soviet Federative Socialist Republic. Immediately following the Great October Revolution, when the Bolshevik party and the workers' soviets seized power, Lenin's vision for the new state included a platform for national self-determination, in part as a way of "courting" non-Russian factions within the new Soviet Union. But self-determination was a complex and contingent idea, and there was no united party line (although there were plenty of strong opinions and ideological debates; see Smith 1999) about what, exactly, it entailed.

The pivots in the Soviet implementation of self-determination played an important role in how Vepsian futures unfolded over the next several decades, as first Leninism and then Stalinism shaped rural, ethnic regions throughout the land. Lenin viewed self-determination as a useful strategy in the Marxist ideological tool kit, because he concluded that "by granting the forms of nationhood, the Soviet state could split the above-class national alliance for statehood" (Martin 2001: 69). His idea of self-determination can also arguably be seen as a strategy aimed at crafting new citizens: peoples who had been marginalized in tsarist Russia and, as a result of their historical experience, felt apathy or even aversion to political consciousness and distrusted both politics and the state. In their case, non-Russian nationalism, as it emerged, was "primarily a response to Tsarist oppression and was motivated by a historically justifiable distrust of Great Russia" (ibid.: 70). Stalin's investment in self-determination aligned with his vision for the development of "backward" regions, preoccupied as he was with underpopulated stretches of Russian land, especially in border regions. In Stalin's vision, "frontier" territories—with the northern stretches of Karelia decidedly falling into that category—fit into the vision of the doctrinal mandate of a network of economic and industrial bases throughout the republics.

At its dawn, the new Soviet state developed a series of measures to boost the economic condition of the national minorities; conjoined with this program was the development of local educational infrastructure in the national languages. This policy led to the development of national minorities' cultural identity within the new Soviet identity—one could imagine this aspirational model as something akin to Russian nesting dolls—and such benevolent "ethnic" politics of the Soviet regime lay the foundation for autonomous regions and republics throughout the USSR. In terms of the scope of self-determination and sovereignty, autonomous republics were, in the four-tiered hierarchy of territories, second only to the 15 "Union" republics. As significant political units, which in turn contained the third and fourth tiers of administrative units—autonomous areas and autonomous districts—autonomous republics allowed for political consolidation of ethnicities that were too "small-numbered" as populations to become Union republics in their own right (Kurs 2001; Smith 1999).

Created in 1923, the Karelian Autonomous Soviet Socialist Republic became one such "second-tier" region, and the Veps discussed in this book became administratively folded into this newly formed KASSR—their centre being the village of Sheltozero, the site of my fieldwork, and the home of the Ethnographic Museum discussed in the introduction (and further discussed throughout the book). Despite the massive reorganization of Soviet territories on a national basis, the Veps remained divided into two administrative factions, just as they had been in tsarist Russia (Kurs 2001), with the second Vepsian district organized around the town of Vinnitsi.

KORENIZATSIYA (KORENIZATION)

By the end of the 1920s, it was clear to the party elites that the emphasis on national self-determination and ethnic identity as the engine for turning previously discriminated-against minorities into new Soviet citizens was rife with tensions and paradoxes, and did not align with the party goals and ideologies. Essentially, the idea of self-determination was at odds with the primary objective of Soviet nation-building, which was based around the consolidation and centralization of power and the unification of various constituent elements of the state. When, a decade after the revolution, the young country faced a grain shortage, this very practical problem, together with the aforementioned ideological issues, led to a shift in the national perspective about the efficacy and desirability of ethnic self-determination, and, in a reversal of policy, the Soviet collectivization of rural areas began.

Part of this shift was a change in politics around language. Siragusa (2012),[4] in her study of Vepsian language and politics, compiles an excellent in-depth history of linguistic interventions and their far-reaching consequences, and discusses these shifts in politics in an ethnohistorical perspective. As she points out, the new set of priorities focused on overcoming rural "backwardness" and "obscurantism" and instilling "culture" throughout regions traditionally considered "uncultured" in the urban-rural dichotomy, which historically located culture and education in cities rather than the countryside, with its decentralized tradition of peasant self-education. *Likbez* (short for *likvidatsiya bezgramotnosti*, or "liquidation of illiteracy") was a campaign to eradicate illiteracy that started immediately after the revolution, assembled by Narkompros, the Soviet Ministry for Education. During the first decade of the Soviet regime, in alignment with the policies of national self-determination, the fight against illiteracy took shape through the training of literacy teachers, who were deployed throughout Soviet territories to educate local populations in locally established, self-determined languages. With the transition from self-determination to collectivization, however, language policies changed as well.[5] Specifically, Narkompros was now guided by the policy of **korenizatsiya**, translated as "indigenization" or "nativization," and literally meaning "putting down roots" (and it should be noted that the term for indigenous peoples in Russian is *korennye narodi*, meaning "rooted peoples"). The policy, somewhat akin to contemporary affirmative action policies in the United States, was designed to promote titular nations within Soviet and autonomous republics, and within the administrative apparatuses of these states, to appoint indigenous people as local bureaucrats, management, and government officials. This policy was supposed to compensate for the historically constituted economic disparity between, to use a World Systems analogy,[6] the peripheries and the centres of the tsarist Russian empire—a disparity that generally went hand in hand with the forced Russification of colonized and oppressed nationalities in imperial Russia. While definitively a pro-indigenous and pro-local culture policy, korenizatsiya marked the shift from a focus on self-determination by ethnic minorities to a focus on nation-building, and effectively incorporating them in that project through maximizing economic and linguistic parity, integrating locals into the government hierarchy, and also encouraging (and in some cases mandating) ethnic Russians who served in local governments to learn local languages and cultures.

Korenizatsiya was made possible by *natsionalno-territorialnoye razmezhevaniye* (national-territorial demarcation), a process of codifying administrative and territorial divisions, in many cases linked to ethnic groups (a.k.a. nations). This was not an easy task, as demarcating a nation or a clear ethnic group was a highly politicized and far from self-evident process in the early Soviet Union—and one that was aided by early Soviet ethnographers.

In line with the general taxonomic approach the Soviet state took to various indigenous and ethnic peoples, the ABCD hierarchy was a system that catalogued and ranked the 120 languages of the Soviet Union, using three basic criteria to distinguish between them (speaker population size, existence or lack of an established orthography, and degree of territorial unity of speakers), and created specific plans for each nation's literacy, grounded in instruction in native language. By 1934, textbooks were being printed in 104 languages (up from 25 languages a mere 10 years earlier) (Grenoble 2006: 46–47).

Beyond the Karelian Republic, the 1930s was in general a period in Soviet history when national territories named after specific peoples (unions and autonomous republics) and national-territorial formations (oblast's, okrugs, and districts) were being created. The basis for the administrative borders of these spaces of minority peoples was the 1926 census. The status of ethno-territorial formations was pursued as a result of the politics of "indigenization" that were in effect in the USSR until the mid-1930s, the goal of which was parity in the political, cultural, and economic development of non-Russian peoples and ethnic minorities. The inequalities between nationalities were meant to be overcome through the formation of interconnected measures, allowances, and privileges, aimed at an accelerated formation of a national elite and a working class. Labour protocols and school curricula were translated into local languages, and educational and cultural programs were conducted in them.

This was designed to facilitate the institutionalization of ethnicities and the growth of national (ethnic) self-awareness of peoples. Within the framework of this politics, the Soviet state had a program for the national-cultural development of the Veps.

Prior to the revolution, Veps were considered to be *osedlye inorodtsi* (resident foreigners), who practiced Christianity and did not have any special legal status as subjects of the Russian empire. During the indigenization politics period, Veps started to be considered as a national minority. This led to the formation of a Vepsian okrug (area) in the Leningradskaya Oblast District, and plans were developed (although not realized) for two Vepsian National Districts in Karelia. At the beginning of the 1930s, Vepsian national cadres were also being prepared for political and cultural-educational work. In 1934, several hundred Vepsian youths started higher education programs. One of the main goals of indigenization politics lay in the liquidation of illiteracy among non-Russian populations through studies in one's own language. The fact that Vepsian had been an oral, rather than a written language, presented a challenge.

For Veps, this policy and its implementation had mixed results. While in Sheltozero and the rest of Vepsian territories within the KASSR, the new language regime meant that Vepsian became the formal language of instruction (in place of Finnish, previously preferred), the Veps "next door" in the Leningradskaya Oblast' were actually stripped of their national status and excluded from the list of nationalities in the 1939 census. As a result, Vepsian as formal language of instruction was actually abolished for the Leningrad Veps (Kurs 2001: 73). This kind of ethnolinguistic fragmentation of what was essentially a topographically continuous indigenous territory was typical of Stalin's policy toward minorities. In some cases, the split was not purely administrative; rather, certain parts of ethnic groups were physically relocated and populations scattered as a measure of top-down control (Anderson 1991, 2000; Reeves 2007).

Such top-down language reform was not the only form of "modernization" that affected Veps in this time period. Soviet "best practices" in agricultural production, as well as urbanization, were transforming the rhythms of village life (Siragusa 2012). For one, human-animal relations were transformed: while historically, Veps had a close connection with animals, especially cattle, as sources of food but also as instruments of labour, the late 1920s and early 1930s saw the very beginning of the aspirational mechanization of the agricultural sector throughout the Soviet republics, with tractors replacing horses (Conquest 1986). While historically almost every household in the Vepsian villages had a cow[7] and a horse, the numbers of animals dwindled in the 1930s and never went up again, despite later efforts at retraditionalization in some other cultural areas. When I was doing fieldwork in Sheltozero, only a few households had a cow, and virtually no one had or used horses; even the older generation of Veps I interviewed, in their 70s now, recalled their youthful days of labour in the field, farming with tractors.

Modernization and mechanization went hand in hand with urbanization, which, in turn, was a trend that was connected with the emphasis on education and literacy. With the possibilities and expectations that education offered, many people moved to Petrozavodsk because of the university located there. At the same time, there was an increase in labour migration among loggers and metalworkers, connected to the construction of the Kirov Railway—one of the early Soviet mega-industrial projects; this brought a number of other ethnic groups to Karelia, including Finns, Belorussians, and Tatars.

THE WAR YEARS

As a border zone, Karelia had a complicated social and political existence during World War II, and Veps, as a minority associated with Finns and claimed by Finns as "their own," were in an unusual and difficult position as a Soviet population, both during and after the war—an important symbolic fixture and memory space in the life of the village of Sheltozero. As I discovered during my research stay, virtually all the elderly people who came of age in Sheltozero had either participated in the war or were affected directly by the military campaigns in the region and the occupation. Thus, this moment in history was either a personal experience for them, or at the very least, powerful family lore.

Life history interviews with village elders illustrate some of the most important ways in which the war affected the village and paint a picture of what life was like after the war, a traumatic time during which the countryside was reorganized, a process that in many ways laid the foundation for the liquidation of villages, like the ones around Sheltozero, that would happen in the next several decades.

One of my interviewees, Anna Ivanovna, spoke about her own experiences and those of her husband, Alexander (to whom she refers as Grandfather during the interview), during the war and the occupation. In the following portion of the interview, she recounts his trajectory, which I include here because it is representative of the older generation's experience. She started her husband's story thus: "Grandfather—he was in the occupation, and I was in the occupation too.... He was 14 then—they took Voznesenie [nearby village that had been liquidated/abandoned after the war]. The Finns got as far as Voznesenie—that's 50 kilometres from here, by the main road."

The Finnish occupation of Karelia is an important chapter in the regional history of the war and border relations. During the Continuation War, the

Finnish Army set up a military administration in Eastern Karelia; it was in operation from summer 1941 until summer 1944. Finland had a mythohistorical kind of interest in the region and aspired to annex it: Eastern Karelia was featured in Finland's national saga, the *Kalevala*—an epic poem assembled in the nineteenth century by Elias Lönnrot, who based it on oral folklore and myths told by rural storytellers—and was considered by the Finns to be the cradle of Finnish culture. Non-Russian Karelians (including Veps) were considered to be "kindred people" who needed to be liberated from Russia. This long-standing mythohistorical interest of Finland in Eastern Karelia was "authenticated" during World War II in a state-sponsored project, when the Finnish government, allied with Germany, was confident of a quick German victory over the Soviet Union. President Risto Ryti commissioned a book titled *Finnlands Lebensraum* (Finland's Living Space), authored by state-comissioned geographer Väinö Auer and historian Eino Jutikkala, who, using Third Reich frontier vocabulary to frame their claim, sought to legitimize through scholarly arguments the conceit that Eastern Karelia naturally constituted a part of Finland's "living space" (Vilén 2013).

The "Karelian issue" was an active one in Finland in the 1920s and 1930s; the idea of reclamation/reunification was a popular ideological platform with university students, and it was further amplified by organizations of East Karelian refugees who crossed the border to escape the communist regime. The Winter War[8] further fuelled anger toward the Soviet state as an oppressive force, and then, finally, as a minor ally of Germany, Finland was in a position to implement their "Greater Finland" vision, which started with the Finnish commander-in-chief, Marshal Mannerheim, issuing an order to begin the occupation, phrased thus:

> In the War of Liberation of 1918 I said to the Karelians of Finland and Eastern Karelians that I would not put my sword back in its scabbard before Finland and Eastern Karelia were free. The freedom of Karelia and a Great Finland are glimmering in front of us in the enormous avalanche of the world historic events. May the Providence that directs the fate of nations allow the Finnish Army to fulfill my pledge to the Karelian people. Soldiers! The earth on which you are about to tread is holy land soaked with the blood and suffering of our people. Your victory will liberate Karelia, your deeds will create a great and happy future for Finland. (Hentilä 1999: 201)

Since the military administration was supposed to be a precursor of eventual annexation and integration into the Finnish state—as a part of the "Greater Finland" vision—the aims and policies of the occupation were different than those in many European territories occupied by the Axis powers (with which Finland was allied as a co-belligerent state). The occupying forces were supposed to build relationships of positive affect with the local population, in tandem with ideological restructuring or "reclaiming." Places that did not already have Finnish or Karelian alternative names (i.e., Sihv for Sheltozero) were renamed, and streets were stripped of their Soviet names and re-christened with the names of Finnish patriots and war heroes, both contemporary (like chief of the military, Mannerheim) and historical (from the *Kalevala*).

Veps were included in the Finnish concept of *heimo*—the "kindred spirits" who were demarcated as such based on a pseudo-scientific anthropology of ethnicity similar to the one used by the Nazis in creating their racial taxonomies. As such, Veps (along with Karelians, Ingrians, and Estonians) belonged to the sector of the population that was being groomed for a reunification with Finland in an imagined future in which Germany would have conquered Russia and the non-heimo contingent (Russians and some Ukrainians and Belorussians) would be expelled from the region.

Anna Ivanovna continued the story of her husband's youth into my voice recorder: "So, he did not go to the Finnish school. Then he was called to the commandant's office, and he was told, "Since you don't go to school, we are not going to leave you here." They were nervous about boys left to their own devices, you see, what they could do if they had a leader. So they sent him to Voznesenie. All the young people who were not in school were in Voznesenie— they worked, mostly dug trenches. And because he was still so young, they made him a bath-boy, he heated bathhouses."

The schools Anna Ivanovna referred to were a part of the Finnish propaganda plan directed at the spread of pan-Finnicism, designed to represent the Finnish military as liberators and to foster antagonism between "nationals" and Russians. As a part of this Finnish nationalizing project, the military established the newspaper *Vapaa Karjala* (Free Karelia), a later newspaper *Paatenen Viesti* (Padan News), and Aunus Radio, all geared at diminishing Russians and praising Finland and Finns (interviews and Verigin 2009).

Altogether, the Finns established over a hundred schools with Finnish-language education throughout the region. Attendance was mandatory for heimo children between the ages of 7 and 15, and both Finnish heroic history and religion were heavily emphasized; the Finns intended to use the region's still prevalent latent religiosity—which was subject to ongoing repression by the socialist Soviet state, for ideological reasons and with the aspiration of eventual eradication—as a way to win local loyalties and foster anti-communist sentiments. This ideological calculation was part of a multi-pronged strategy to build rapport with the local populations, especially the young Veps, who, presumably, could be easily won over and indoctrinated. In his memoir, *Detstvo Opalennoye Voynoy* (*Childhood Singed by the War*) (2004b), Ryurik Lonin, the founder of the Sheltozero museum, describes his experiences as a schoolboy in one such school under the occupation. First of all, he explained that the Finnish schoolteacher facilitated pen-pal relationships between the Vepsian schoolchildren and their Finnish counterparts:

> Before the start of the first class, Selma addressed us: "Kids, I brought from Finland addresses of your age-peers. Who would like to be penpals with them? I will copy down their addresses for you." Many wanted to participate, and the teacher handed out the addresses of Finnish schoolchildren. It was distributed in such a way that each boy received an address of a Finnish girl, and each of our girls—the address of a Finnish boy. The next day I wrote to "my" girl a letter in Vepsian, and soon thereafter received a reply. In her short reply, the girl wrote: "Hello, Yuuri (that's what I was called in the Finnish school), I received your letter. Thank you. There is grief in our family: my mom died. I feel very sorry for her. I cried so hard at the funeral." That was the end of the letter…soon I wrote her another letter but never received a response. She probably did not understand Vepsian language very well, and I did not yet know Finnish that well. (p. 41, my translation)

Lonin also recounted the role of the schools in ensuring good nutrition for children and teens in the occupied territory. As he explained in the memoir, school grounds were refashioned into garden plots where students grew vegetables for their households, with seeds handed out by teachers: carrots, beets, turnips. He also wrote, "They gave us free hot lunches at school, and in those days, when all the food was strictly rationed by cards, and rations were small, they were quite filling" (p. 41). School was used as a centre for distributing supplies of margarine, confiscated from Soviet food pantries, to the parents of Vepsian students. Beyond the food, Finnish educators were the source of presents: "We long recalled with my friends how on the eve of the 1943 New Year, Grandfather Frost came into the classroom with a full bag and said to us: 'Kids, I came here straight from Lapland, where I have permanent residency, like all the other Grandfather Frosts. And here, I brought presents for you. They were collected for you by Finnish schoolchildren' … the bag turned out to contain dolls, toy monkeys, horses on wheels, and other stuff" (47).

These incentives were coupled with the methodical de-Russification of school territory. As Lonin recounted, on the first day of Finnish school, the teacher commanded, "Children, take out all the Russian books and notebooks out onto the street, we are going to burn them" (29–30). While the trope of domination and occupation enacted through the burning of books and suppression of the communication culture of subjects considered to be in opposition to the goals of those in power is a familiar one, enacted throughout Nazi Europe, in the case of Soviet Veps, such book-burnings had a complicated nuance to them. In sense, these acts of repression overwrote previous acts of repression by the Soviet state. Bonfires of Soviet textbooks mapped onto the prohibition of Vepsian language in 1937, pitting Vepsian identities as Soviet citizens against their cultural and ethnic (and linguistic) personhood.

Altogether, for the Veps in the region, the experience of the Finnish occupation was a complicated one, rife with ambiguities and contradictions stemming from Vepsian positionality vis-à-vis the Soviet state. As Lonin summed up in his memoir (which obviously would not have been possible to publish during the Soviet era), "In my recollections, I do not praise the Finnish occupation on our Vepsian land, but I am not trying to thicken the paint, either.... It is appropriate to quote a book published in Finland in 2002 in the publishing house Atena, by Mauno Yokipp. It is called *Baltic-Finnish Peoples. History and Dates of Kindred Peoples*. Page 301: 'Finns treated their brothers by blood with a benevolent disposition, and made sure they were well fed, almost as well as their own countrymen, despite production difficulties—but they were strict about discipline'" (Lonin 2004b: 42).

Returning to "Grandfather," who is the main protagonist of this chapter, as a part of this discipline, as a Veps (that is, a "national"), Anna Ivanovna's husband was ordered to attend such a school; at the same time, because he was a national, his refusal carried lighter consequences than non-compliance would have for a non-national—essentially, he was attached to a labour brigade in a place where "re-education" was going on even outside the school context.

The next chapter of young Grandfather's life involved a planned population transfer and the subsequent return. As Anna Ivanovna narrated,

And then when the Finns left, they took all the youth with them to Finland, on a fleet of trucks, with Finns guarding them with automatic weapons, so that they wouldn't jump out and run. One ran, and they shot him. I don't know what their goal was, why they took the youth to Finland. They transported them in the cars, then they walked on foot ... and they were in Finland for several months ... and then—well, you know, it's all politics, we don't quite understand it, but there was an agreement, that the Finnish prisoners of war would be returned to Finland, and then this— our—youth would be returned. Some stayed—they changed their last name quickly— for example, got married ... even during the occupation, a few women here married Finns—well, but those were rare instances. And then our Russian officers said to the youth, "You are going home." The Finns wanted to keep them there but these kids decided they needed to go home, and that's that. Of course in Finland they were well dressed, and they weren't hungry ... but still. The brigade where Grandfather was, near Veyznu, just 10 kilometres away—they missed them in the exchange at first. Then they found out that all the other Russian brigades were already transported back—and how did they get left behind? They found a Russian officer, and said, "We are still here," so he of course made arrangements. So they returned to Russia.

Anna Ivanovna may not have known why Finns took the "national" population with them when they retreated, but it was all a part of the Suur-Suomi, the "Greater Finland," program. The Finns were already anxious about demographic issues of underpopulation and set about completing large-scale population transfers in the border region and within the occupied territories. While plans were in place to repopulate Eastern Karelia with "nationals" consolidated from other regions,[9] the infrastructure of large-scale population transfers also served the Finnish goal of taking "their" people with them when they were pushed back; the plan was to continue re-educating Vepsian youth, integrate them into Finnish society, and have them settle on the Finnish side of the Eastern Karelia region.

Although in the regional historical narratives, the local youths' resistance to the transport and the desire to go home was often cast as evidence of genuine communist sentiments and political commitments, the more accurate explanation generally had to do with the fact that these young men and women (mostly men) were eager to go home and be reunited with their families, with whom they had had no contact across the occupation lines for several years. As another woman whom I interviewed, whose brother was a part of this "youth transfer" said, "When he came back, he told us he had tried running away twice, he was so worried about us—it was just my mother and my sisters, our papa was *na fronte* [at the front lines, in the military], of course, and he was worried how the household would be, without a man. Papa told him, before he left us, that he was the man now, he had to take care of us— and then just like that, for two years, he did not know what was happening, if we were starving, nothing."

The homecoming of Vepsian youth was, however, not what they expected, as Anna Ivanovna's husband, Alexander, found out firsthand:

They thought they were going home—but instead, right away they were sent to the Velikholukskaya Oblast', to a kolkhoz [a collective farm]. Of course, it was famine there, people are starving, and here they come, they are not even dressed properly, they are wearing light shoes.... And you know, when they were leaving, the Finns said, "Guys, take some clothes, and take some food with you, you will be starving as soon as you get there." I guess they knew, the Finns. And us, we didn't know—there was no communication with families, even though it was not that far. So they were sent straight there—they were freezing, cold, covered in lice—and they ran away. On foot, hiding in cargo trains.... More than once militia caught them, returned them to the kolkhoz, but a few of them, including Grandfather, made it home, back to Petrozavodsk, back to Karelia. He came home, knocked on the door early in the morning—he tried to walk only during the night, so that he would not be caught and returned—they did not have any documents, of course, they could have been put in prison … and many were put in prison, when they returned from Finland— prisons and labour camps. And people were dying, for no reason. People were not to blame for anything—the politicians decided everything. But it was not their fault that they got captured! So many people suffered, so many Vepsian families suffered.

Veps were already ethnically "suspect" in Stalin's book—according to Shearer (2006: 211), "As the 1930s wore on, Stalin came to mistrust certain … ethnic groups, which he suspected of having potential loyalties outside the U.S.S.R." Veps were included in Stalin's purges and large-scale repressions because of their close association with Finns.[10] Anna Ivanovna recalls her own and her husband's Vepsian peers, who suffered the same fate as many Soviet prisoners of war and found themselves arrested and subjected to punitive measures as a consequence of having been captured. Her husband's labour assignment was not punitive in the same way, but it was part of the Soviet massive reorganization of the rural countryside, and of agricultural production; Alexander was assigned to a kolkhoz (a type of Soviet collective farm) on the basis of labour and demographic needs. While a kolkhoz was not a Gulag (forced labour camp), kolkhoz populations were tethered to their places of labour; they were not issued passports, and their ability to move and find work elsewhere was curtailed. In a way, the Veps of the region attached to these collective farms were circumscribed in movements and life choices in a way that was reminiscent of their tenure as "state peasants" during the time of Peter the Great. The kolkhoz system, though, was more porous than the penal system, since its members were not prisoners, and escapes, such as Alexander's, were possible.

"So he came home," Anna Ivanovna continues, "knocked on the door, his own mother did not recognize him. She said, 'I don't know who came here.' And he said, 'It's me, mama, it's me.' She started crying—'Come into the house, quickly.' 'Better run a bath,' he said. 'I am covered in lice.' And then … of course he still could not get any documents; he went to work for a kolkhoz here, no passport—they did not give passports to *kolkhozniki*…. My mama was like that—she lived without a passport till she was 70. All her life she lived without a passport—so she could not leave, so she would support the kolkhoz, winter in the kolkhoz, summer in the kolkhoz. For five years, all they got was a bag of rye and a hundred rubles. For five years! And in the winter they were sent to do logging—and logging back then was … just with an axe. No mechanization. So they suffered in the forests, Grandfather cut down wood, and then transported it by horse."

Collectivization of village life transformed Vepsian communities in a dramatic way—the long-established system of kin-based field and forest entitlements was dismantled beyond recognition. The village demographics had already been dramatically changed by the war: many men had died, and some had remained in Finland. Further inter- and intra-regional migration followed World War II. After the fragmentation and the rapid and often violent restructuring that followed in Vepsian villages after the war, the 1950s, 1960s, and 1970s saw Veps in general follow the larger Soviet trend of, first, population transfers in the service of collectivization, then village liquidation and urbanization.

Although the Soviet Union was 99 per cent collectivized[11] by 1937, the demographic shifts brought about by World War II meant that people were deployed to collective farms that were not necessarily in their own region or republic. And just a decade later, Vepsian livelihoods, along with the liveli-hoods of other rural peoples of Russia, were restructured by Nikita Kruschev, the first general secretary of the Soviet Union after the long reign of Joseph Stalin. Kruschev, as a part of a series of multi-pronged economic and polit-ical reforms, launched a project geared at urbanization and the liquidation of villages. At the twenty-second Party Congress in 1961, Khrushchev expressed the intention and the plan to build communism in the coming 20 years—an aspiration which was parlayed into the Third Program[12] of the Communist Party of the Soviet Union—and massive infrastructure projects (buildings commonly known as *khrushevki*, after the prime minister's name) were built around urban perimeters. These multi-storey residential buildings, made of prefabricated concrete panels or brick, were designed to solve "the housing problem" and to accommodate the redistribution of labour power, primarily toward urban areas (Grandstaff 1980). Like all urban centres, Petrozavodsk had a building boom, where clusters of such buildings were erected to accom-modate a large-scale population transfer, which would include many Veps, from the neighbouring rural countryside into the city.

Although the aim of centralizing collective farming (turning the kolkhozes, or collective farms, into the bigger sovkhozes, or state farms) was to maxi-mize production, the result was in fact its loss—farming became less efficient and the land located beyond the easy reach of the new sovkhozes was aban-doned. Pockets of farmland between areas of swamp and forest, which had been cultivated and used as pasture for centuries, were now left to grow wild.

The villages were classified into two categories: *perspektivnye* (those with prospects) and *neperspektivnye* (those without prospects). Those villages regarded as being without prospects stopped being provided with any invest-ment in public services and infrastructure (Kurs 2001: 73). Once the collec-tive farm closed, the money allocated for roadworks, as well as electrical grids and plumbing systems in the village would be reallocated to the villages "with prospects." This closure of the farm and subsequent diversion of state funds would make the village increasingly less viable. Without state support, schools, public cafeterias, post offices, and stores would close, and at some point electricity and water systems would be dismantled, and the residents would be resettled in blocks of flats on the outskirts of nearby urban centres, or in larger villages "with prospects." The implementation of this policy affected the traditional lifestyle of Veps (and other village dwellers in Russia) irrevers-ibly (Strogalshikova 2008a, 2008b). It amplified, and in some cases caused, migration to urban areas and made remaining villages larger (as smaller villages were consolidated into larger units that could be classified as "with prospects") and farther apart from each other. This regional rural-to-urban migration overlapped with an influx of migrant workers from other parts of the Soviet Union. Tatars, Armenians, Ukrainians, and Belorussians in partic-ular flocked to Karelia, to the border region, after being recruited as a labour force. These simultaneous and multiple social forces changed regional demo-graphics, subsistence practices, and language use. Russian was the dominant language in cities, particularly in urban workplaces, and migration to cities drove mixed marriages between Veps and non-Veps, as did the deployment of sovkhoz organizers to the villages.[13] As was pointed out to me, either as explicit data or simply mentioned casually with regret in conversations about family history, for a number of decades—in fact, until the recent linguistic revival—such mixed marriages virtually ensured that the next generation of children would grow up speaking Russian rather than Vepsian.

While it seemed inevitable that Veps, a particularly tiny minority group, would be all but completely assimilated in terms of cultural and linguistic practices by the end of the Soviet era, Vepsian culture proved to be resilient. While the rest of this book's chapters focus on various aspects of the ethno-graphic realities of Vepsian life today, there is another short but very impor-tant chapter in the ethnohistorical overview of Vepsian culture—one that can, perhaps, be viewed as a distillation of Veps' understanding of themselves and their history at the beginning of the twenty-first century, and the ways in which they are vulnerable to economic exploitation and concomitant forms of dispos-session against the backdrop of the post-Soviet era of ever-escalating privati-zation and neoliberalization of a resource-driven economy.

A BRIEF HISTORY OF THE SHORT-LIVED VEPSIAN
NATIONAL VOLOST'

The ethnographic museum has a dedicated corner that features a flag: a cross of blue and yellow across a green background. Blue is for the water of lakes and rivers, yellow is for sunlight, green is for grass and forest. It is the flag of the Vepsian National Volost' which was formed on January 20, 1994 by an edict of the Supreme Council of the Republic of Karelia. The formation of the Volost' was a late entry in the early post-Soviet phenomenon known as "the parade of sovereignties," a period that started after a speech Boris Yeltsin made in the city of Ufa, commenting on new legislation that elevated republic rights over soyuz rights. In that speech, Yeltsin famously quipped to the republics, "Take as much sovereignty as you can swallow!"

The Volost' was designed to be a self-governing territory incorporating Shoksha, Sheltozero, and Rybreka, as well as the territory of Kvartiztny, a Soviet-era industry town built to service the quarries, and comprising 13 communities altogether. Sheltozero served as the administrative centre of the Volost'. The political and symbolic import of this decision cannot be overstated. Many of my informants (one of whom, a Vepsian woman from Sheltozero, who wrote her master's thesis at Petrozavodsk State University about the formation of the Volost') recalled the hopeful and aspirational ethos that surrounded this political process, and a jubilant, aspirational sense of the Volost' as being simultaneously a space for a hopeful future and a compensation for the sorts of marginalization experienced by Veps in the past.

Figure 1.2 Vepsian national flag

During its brief existence, the Volost' produced significant and long-lasting effects in terms of Vepsian cultural revival and survival. That fact is not disputed and is, in fact, commemorated on the official history website of the Karelian government as an achievement and a foundation for future cultural revival activities. There the Vepsian History section[14] details the formation of the Volost', noting that it enabled an institutional push toward recreating Vepsian written language, with a number of textbooks and dictionaries being published and, from 1994 on, *Kodima* (Native Land), a bilingual Russian and Vepsian monthly newspaper. In parallel with this linguistic amplification, schools within the Volost' integrated Vepsian language into their curriculum, even as Karelian universities developed infrastructure for training schoolteachers in Vepsian language and started offering courses in Vepsian linguistics and Vepsian language pedagogy practicums. One of my informants, Pavel, told me, "It raised our own consciousness and esteem, for so long it was like, 'Veps, well, they are Veps, they are not needed.' But then Vepsian language being taught in schools, that became a way to pass our traditions to our children and grandchildren outside of just the family, and also they fixed up the House of Culture up the road, and television crews even came several times, and filmed the village—from that bank of the river, right over there. After that, our village was featured in the credits for an evening news show on Karelian television."

The financial administration of the Volost' (according to my aforementioned informant who wrote her thesis on the Volost' formation, and was herself involved in administration and governance during its existence) was designed through a republic-level program called RESURS (a Russian acronym similar to the word for "resource"), developed by the Ministry of Economics of Karelia. The goal of the program was to balance the budget of the Volost' so that it could become self-financing and so that its existence would not be a financial burden on the republic. The key aspect of the program involved creating a "hospitable environment" for industries operating on the territories of the Volost'—primarily logging and mining—and though the Volost' existed only briefly, the "hospitality" to extractive industries that was tethered to its formation outlasted it and played an important role in the deregulation that is the focus of the later chapters of this book.

In a sense, those few years represented a halcyon moment in Vepsian history and their understanding of their own history; their indigenous identity suddenly became a leverage for political sovereignty, which was financed by industries that have historically held a lot of cultural capital and social benefits for Veps, as will be discussed later in the book. As part of the symbolic and the semiotic work of this socio-political Vepsian Renaissance, Vepsian activist Alexie

Maximov, in collaboration with renowned ethnographer of Vepsian ethography and ethnohistory Irina Vinokurova, initiated a project to design a coat of arms for the Volost'. As the project's mission stated,

> The project of the Coat of Arms of Vepsian National Volost' is a shield, with a gold field and tip, formed by four blue and silver undulating stripes. In the gold field, there is a red rooster, holding in front of it a green shamrock. The rooster has silver eyes and talons. The shield is crowned with a silver and gold top in the shape of a Northern Vepsian volute casing. The symbolism is as follows: the red rooster has long been an emblem of the Vepsian holiday "Tree of Life" and has been an unofficial symbol of Onega Veps for many years. The rooster (*kukoi*) has been traditionally honoured by Veps as a domestic protector, and represents the struggle against forces of darkness. In the coat of arms, the red rooster is a symbol of cleansing and spiritual revival. The shamrock ... symbolizes three national village councils: Shoksha, Sheltozero, and Rybreka, united in 1994 into the Vepsian National Volost'. The blue and silver undulating stripes at the bottom of the shield represent the waters of Lake Onega. The gold field stands for stability and wisdom. The crown as an attribute of a self-governing territory represents a particular status of the parish as a national unit within a municipality.[15]

But the coat of arms was never adopted. More importantly, the budget was never balanced. Officials claim that the dissolution of the Volost' on January 1, 2006 was due to its financial insolvency and inability to support itself. Local Veps, who were actively involved in politics around the formation of the Volost', posit a different cause-and-effect relationship. A prevalent belief among many in Sheltozero and surrounding villages is that the logging and the mining industries were so profitable and so mired in corrupt business dealings on the level of the republic that allocating a sum from those profits to subsidize long-term functioning of the Volost' was not a favourable outcome for Karelian politicians, who stood to benefit from the "hospitable conditions" created for the private mining and logging companies rapidly spreading through the area. And, several informants told me, the lack of a balanced budget then became an "excuse" to dissolve the municipality, effectively routing profits from resource extraction in the region well beyond the borders of Vepsian villages. The dissolution of the Volost' after its brief existence was emotionally difficult for the residents of the villages for whom this political shift was, as the museum director told me, "their all"—a synthesis of cultural pride and political activism, and a sense of change and possibility that was quashed when the briefly granted autonomy was taken away.

Veps did not forget about it, though. The existence of the Volost', although brief, crystallized for Veps—and for those who want to learn about them—many central aspects of what is at stake for them as an indigenous minority in the post-Soviet political and economic landscape. The entitlements that were the idealistic basis for the advocacy that shaped the Volost' in the first place were grounded in not only historical identity and pride in culture and language but also natural resources as a historic provider of links of prosperity and respect between Vepsian communities and the state. Natural resources, finally, were going to be leveraged for explicit sovereignty. But it can be argued (and is argued by Vepsian intellectuals in Petrozavodsk and Vepsian villagers alike) that it was the financial promise of those same natural resources that resulted in the Volost' being "yanked away" (as my landlord put it) almost as soon as it came into being. In many ways, the aspects of Vepsian history and culture explored in the subsequent chapters show how this triangulation between Veps, their natural resources, and state authorities has been a defining force in Vepsian history for centuries.

Notes

1. The Russian term for governorate is *gubernia*, and it was the main administrative subdivision of the Russian empire.

2. A name for a settlement in Russia, derived from the Russian word for "freedom"—*svoboda*—meaning a free settlement; the name was changed to Petrozavodsk during Catherine the Great's municipal reform some decades later, in 1777.

3. An administrative region in the former USSR and in its constituent republics.

4. This overview of the history of linguistic policies draws on the aforementioned work with Siragusa (2012) as well as personal correspondence with her, and is augmented with information from interviews with Vepsian linguists on faculty at the Karelian Academy of Sciences.

5. Stalin (1913) authored a seminal work on the subject, entitled "Marxism and the National Question," which formed the basis of the Soviet policy on this subject. Stalin defined a "nation" as "a historically constituted, stable community of people, formed on the basis of a common language, territory, economic life, and psychological makeup manifested in a common culture." Early Soviet ethnographers, operating within the parameters of Marxist ideology, were tasked with establishing which nations met and which nations did not meet these criteria, based on data about their cultural, linguistic, and religious details, as well as the evidence of a present or absent political consciousness of themselves as a "nation." Ethnographers were also involved in developing written alphabets and school systems for many small ethnic groups during the korenizatsiya process (Tishkov 1997).

6. The World Systems Theory is a macrosociological framework for analysing global capitalist economic relations, proposed by Immanuel Wallerstein. Wallerstein proposed that the world was divided into "core" countries: namely, European countries, which had benefited from the colonial imperial enterprise and established themselves as capital-producing strongholds, and "periphery" countries, which had been disadvantaged as colonies and relegated to producing cheap labour and raw materials to help "core" countries grow their wealth.

7. In fact, as we will see in Chapter 2, some of the central Vepsian magical practices revolved around cowherding.

8. The Winter War, also known as the Russo-Finnish War, was a war that the Soviet Union waged against Finland at the beginning of World War II, between November 30, 1939 and March 12, 1940.

9. The other main group intended to be settled in Eastern Karelia were the Ingrian Finns of the Leningradskaya Oblast'.

10. The census carried out in 1939, right after Stalin's mass purges, showed that the Vepsian population had dropped from 24,186 in 1926 to 15,571 in the Leningradskaya Oblast', where Stalinist repression was stronger, as the war had taken a harsher toll there, while the number had risen from 8,587 to 9,388 in Karelia. However, it should be noted that the Vepsian rural population had dropped both in Karelia and the Leningradskaya Oblast', from 8,474 to 6,504, and from 24,045 to 14,424 respectively (Strogalshikova 2008b; Siragusa 2012). In addition to the human victims, Vepsian writing was banned at the height of Stalinist terror in 1937.

11. Meaning that the land tenure and allocation was administrated exclusively through a system of collective or state farms, rather than individual land titles.

12. "Program" in this case refers to the strategic plan for the Communist Party of the Soviet Union, both domestic and international. The first Program dated back to 1903 and was designed to abolish tsarist rule and transfer power and the means of production to the proletariat; the second Program was implemented in 1917, after the October Revolution, with the agenda of building socialism in the new country; and the aforementioned third Program, adopted in 1961, was a vision of building communism over the next 20 years.

13. This was the case with my landlord and my landlady. He was a Veps, and she had come to Sheltozero in the 1960s as part of a Komsomol (Soviet political youth group organization, abbreviation for All-Union Leninist Young Communist League) initiative to "build a sovkhoz." They got married, so she stayed.

14. http://www.gov.karelia.ru/Power/Committee/National/vepsy.html.

15. From the website of the Russian Centre of Vexillology and Heraldry, http://www.heraldicum.ru/russia/subjects/towns/veps.htm.

CHAPTER 2

VEPSIAN COSMOLOGIES

In front of the Sheltozero ethnographic museum stands a wooden sculpture carved out of a tree trunk—Lesovik, or **Leshiy** (creature of the forest, male-gendered), another word for Khozyain (Master), the forest spirit central to Vepsian beliefs, and, consequently, to Vepsian spiritual and even linguistic practices. Early in my stay in Sheltozero, I remarked to Nataliya Ankhimova, the director of the museum, that in a way the statue was the first thing one saw that indicated entering Sheltozero. Although the museum was situated a few hundred metres down the road from the Sheltozero sign, the road sign was of an unremarkable blink-and-you-will-miss-it variety, with the subsequent stretch not really different from the interstitial space between the villages that preceded it: a river and a ravine on the right, patches of fields on the left, a building that was once a store but has been lost to time and is now a slowly deteriorating wooden structure. Then, right after a curve in the road, the museum sails into view, with the sculpture of the Master right in front of it as its harbinger. Nataliya replied, half jokingly, half seriously, "Well, of course. It lets you know right away where you have arrived: you are in Sheltozero, and it's the Master's land. The Master is the Master of the museum, too, because the museum is the centre of our culture."

This chapter provides an overview of the Veps' forest-related cosmology of Masters (Khozyayeva in plural form); the symbolism and the practices of this belief system is crucial not only to understanding Vepsian ideas about relationships between humans and nature but also to understanding how they conceptualize relationships to power and authority. As will become clear in this chapter, and throughout the book, historically Veps have always imagined links between their forest spirits and that other order of Masters: human actors in positions of political and economic power.

A NOTE ON CHRISTIANITY

While the majority of the cosmological focus in my ethnography focuses on the folk beliefs around regulatory spirits, those beliefs must be contextualized within the religious context of Russian Orthodox Christianity, into which Veps were converted around the eleventh century. As ethnohistorian Lyudmila Koroleva (n.d.) notes in an essay featured on the website of the Russian Museum of Ethnography in St. Petersburg, the conversion of the Veps "was necessary for neutralizing Swedish influence in the region, and slowing down the spread of Catholicism in the East. In the first half of the XIII century [this region] was already paying a church tithe. The introduction of the new religion aided the process of ethnic consolidation [of Vepsian communities]." Vinokurova (2003) notes that early assimilation into Christianity shaped the subsequent iterations of the few world-origin myths Veps possessed, with the creation of the universe attributed to the Christian figures of the God and the Devil. As she points out, although Veps did not retain a strong body of mythology, the belief in forest spirits that is central to this book, and this chapter in particular, persisted over the centuries and became interwoven with Christianity. It is important to stress, though, that Veps are religious, practicing Christians. Historically, after the conversion, every Vepsian village had at least one small altarless chapel (often erected, as was explained to me, in response to, or anticipation of, some sort of misfortune, whether agricultural, or epidemiological) where villagers themselves held services. Today, one of the most visually notable buildings in Sheltozero is the church with its bright blue cupolas.

Veps go to services on Sundays, whenever possible, and celebrate religious holidays. I happened to be in Sheltozero over Easter and was delighted by the abundance of the festively decorated Easter eggs in people's homes. It should also be noted that in addition to the long-established dominance of Russian Orthodox Christianity in the spiritual lives of Veps, aesthetics and landmark history play a role in the importance of Christianity to Veps' sense and appreciation of their own history. It is important to note that the region around Lakes Onega and Ladoga is famous throughout Russia for its concentration of wooden churches that epitomize the Old Russian architecture and building tradition that flourished in Central and Northern Russia from the fifteenth century on. Cracraft (1988: 39) notes the importance of such architecture to the Russian national project and pride: "The dominant nationalist tendency in Russian architectural historiography insists that ... Old Russian Architecture is distinguished by its generally high standards, both aesthetic and technical ... as reflected for instance in a work published in 1889 by V. Suslov, Academician of Architecture. 'Appointed by the Imperial Academy of Fine Art to study monuments of our old art, Suslov reported to the Academy, he turned first to the wooden churches of the North, since he considered them to embody not only beauty and technical sophistication but an 'immediate expression of the national genius.'" Though revered as relics of Russian architecture and art, these churches are sources of deep appreciation and pride for Veps as well, since on Vepsian territories many of them were constructed, either partially or as a whole, by Vepsian woodworkers, who, as we will see in Chapter 5, incorporated aesthetic details and motifs of Vepsian symbology and material culture into the design of the churches. As we have already seen, it is part of the historically constituted cultural experience of Northern Veps to take pride in their crafts, and although church construction is not as primary to their identity as work with decorative minerals (described in Chapter 3), it still maps onto a sensibility that recognizes and values artifacts of Vepsian artisanal labour in the region, especially when it is rescaled to the level of national value, as happened with the wooden churches.

MASTERS AS REGULATORY FORCES

"The forest folk"—a name attributed to Veps by their Russian neighbours—is one with which they self-identify. It would be difficult to overstate the importance and centrality of the forest to the Vepsian cosmology. While the traditional beliefs of Veps pivot around Khozyayeva of different domains, both outside and inside the home (water, field, the house itself, stove, stable, barn, bathhouse, and well), the central figure in this metaphysical landscape is the Master of the Forest, a crossover figure in Russian and Veps folklore, also known as Leshiy, or *izand*[1] (in the Vepsian language). Veps themselves predominantly use the term Khozyain, although Leshiy is also not uncommon usage. In Vepsian lore, the Khozyain could manifest in the guise of an animal, usually a bear.[2] But more frequently he is thought to appear as a man of various ages and heights—a short old man "the height of the juniper" or a young man as tall "as the tallest trees" (Azovskaya 1977: 147)—always wearing a coat with the left front flap overlapping the right, and a red sash. The concept of the Masters has been written about a lot in ethnographies and histories of post-Soviet territories; they populate Russian and North/Inner Asian landscapes. A non-exhaustive list includes *ezen* (spirit masters) among the Duha of Northern Mongolia (Kristensen 2007); *ezed* and *badagshin* among the Darhad Mongols, also of Northern Mongolia (Pedersen 2007); *cher eezi* in Tyva (Purzycki 2010); and *ee* in Altai. The latter is a term which "is often translated into Russian as khozyain meaning master/landlord/owner but when paired with words like water, land, mountain, it refers to the master spirits of the particular entity" (Broz 2007: 296): an "ownership" structure identical to the one used among Veps (as opposed to other systems of Mastery, where Masters may own specific game animals, for instance). The notion of spirit masters found in and associated with the natural realm is not unique to Eastern Europe or Central Asia, either. One need only look at Amazonian literature, for example (Walker 2012; Descola 2012), for ethnographic insight into cultures where spiritual mastery, much as in the case of the Veps, creates a system of spiritual governance of forests, waterways, and, at times, different orders of plants and animals. As anthropologist Fausto (2012: 35) wrote about the Amazon, but could have written about many other cultures, including Veps, "Informing human action over what we call the natural world is [the idea] that everything has or can have an owner." In virtually all these cases, including that of Veps, looking at the lore of the Masters, and the kinds of rules that people follow in their relationships with them or their domains, reveals a lot about how a given culture understands ideas of reciprocity, respect, transgression, and the like. And as this chapter will show, the different kinds of owners—in the spiritual, political, or even commercial realms—can be thought of as "mirroring" each other. They may be different figures, some conceptualized as entities one encounters in the forest, some clearly identified as captains of industries or rulers of the land, but in the Vepsian world view, every realm, every domain, has a figure of a Master or an Owner. And when Masters or Owners (of any kind) are present, one can and must enter into careful negotiation with them, as they are charged with ensuring that any kind of social or economic transaction that takes place is done in a way that Veps understand to be proper or fair.

Anthropologist Douglas Rogers, who conducted fieldwork in the town of Sepych, in the Ural Mountains, encountered the concept of a Khozyain as a political idea, as his ethnographic subjects, owners of a former state farm turned joint stock company, navigated the early post-Soviet economic landscape. Exploring this topic through the figure of a charismatic Khozyain, the long-time director of the state farm, Rogers posed a series of questions about the very nature of a Khozyain, and his questions are relevant to this ethnography as well. As will become clear throughout the book, for the Veps, Khozyayeva [plural] as a class are their forest spirits—they are also state authorities, and, more recently, foreign owners of stone quarries on Vepsian territories. But this chapter deals with them as spiritual entities, as it is Vepsian belief in Forest Masters that over time has become applied to their understanding of the social and political relationships they are involved in.

Rogers (2006: 915) asked, "What qualities did a proper Khozyain possess? What capabilities and actions were good evidence of one's status as a Khozyain? What domains did various Khozyayeva command, how, and to what effect?" I took a page from his ethnography, which I had read shortly before departing for my fieldwork, and tried to find out the answers to these questions in the context of Vepsian communities; I also tried to find out what Veps believe happens to the Forest Masters when the forests they inhabit become transformed in ways Veps have no control over. This is something I discuss in greater depth in Chapter 5.

The Master of the Forest, in Vepsian cosmology, has the power to send game to a hunter, or mushrooms and berries to gatherers, and to protect the cows of a cowherder; but he is frequently a punitive actor as well, punishing transgressions. These functions do not contradict each other: spirit Khozyayeva comprise a single class across their respective domains (forest, lake, house, and the aforementioned others), and actions that might be construed as benevolence or malevolence are equally part of their regulatory functions. The most common punishment doled out by the Forest Master involved becoming "caught on a bad footprint"[3]—a phenomenon both prominently featured in Vepsian lore and reported in first-person narratives by my informants. This entails becoming lost and disoriented in the forest, even in an area that one is very familiar with, and going around in what appear to be circles. A common scenario involves the lost person wandering around in a trance, sometimes for days, and emerging from the forest in an unlikely, remote spot, sometimes one that would seem impossible to reach, with no recollection of where they had been or how they got to the place where they were finally found. Stories about such experiences clearly illustrate the power dynamic between the Masters and the humans in the forest: the forest is understood to be the Master's domain, and any kind of violation—including spitting or littering or being loud, but also any arrogance or presumption of autonomy—is punished. For instance, there is a strong belief that it is forbidden to say "I will be right back" or to indicate any other kind of a clear plan when embarking on a trip to the forest, because such articulations are arrogant: they presume to know how things will unfold in the forest, where only the Khozyain has full mastery over space and time. Such arrogance is immediately punished by a dramatic rearrangement of the transgressor's experience of both space and time, as can be seen in the following examples, drawn from my interviews.

One of my informants, 82-year-old Nikolai Rastvorov, resident of Vekhruchey, a village north of Sheltozero, described two incidents of such spatial and temporal "reorganization": one about a woman from his own village, the other about a Sheltozero woman he encountered as a young tractor operator:

> This woman took her cow outside the village, and she said, "I will just see the cow off, and I will be right back." Well, she went down the hill—and that's it. The cow joined its herd, and the woman—was missing for three days. Later they asked her where she was, and she said "I don't know, I just walked and walked"… she didn't even know day from night, it was never night in her mind.

Another time I was working in the fields [25 kilometres from Sheltozero] and a woman from Sheltozero comes out of the forest.... I couldn't believe my eyes.... She asks "Where am I?" and I say, "Dear, where are you from?" And she says, "From Sheltozero." I say "Sheltozero? How did you get here?" "I just walked and walked." I asked, "How did you cross the rivers? There is more than one river between here and there"—and, you see, there are no bridges over the rivers on that route. And she says, "I didn't see any rivers." See how it is? She can't explain it—she didn't see any rivers! And the rivers are here, to this day.... And she didn't notice that she somehow crossed them.

Another informant, 83-year-old Valentina, told me of an experience she had when she was 14:

One day with my aunt, we went to the *pokos* [the clearing in the forest where villagers scythe hay].... We finished up loading the hay onto her buggy, and she says to me, "The sun is setting, let's go back together." "That's all right," I said. "I will come back right away, right after you." "Right away"—that was not allowed to be said. I loaded up my own buggy, and the horse will not move. It stands up on hind legs, but won't go. And then an [endless] forest of thin aspens [the Leshiy's tree] is being shown to me, many many many aspens, so straight, so thin, not thick, so many of them. And the horse won't go. I started crying.... [Later] my mother and grandmother told me, the Leshiy did that to you, because you said "right away." Should not have said those words.

In some cases, my interviewees reported a "warning" rather than a punishment. Misha, a local hunter, fisherman, and jack-of-all-trades, told me of a time he also momentarily found himself in a supernatural aspen grove while hunting with a friend; they took it as a warning to abandon the hunt for the day, and Misha left the forest "crossing myself all the way out." This last detail is characteristic of the fluid fusion between Christianity and belief in the spirits among the Veps: on the one hand, Christian practices (praying, crossing oneself, holy water) could be used to get some protection from a Master's displeasure, but on the other hand, many Vepsian rituals are obviously syncretic, drawing on Christian traditions and pagan beliefs in tandem, to the same end. For example, before letting the cows out to pasture, Vepsian villagers would both sprinkle holy water on the animals, and pray to the Apostles to keep them safe—but also try to secure protection for them through the kinds of contracts and offerings with the Forest Master, as described later in this chapter.

Misha also recounted several incidents experienced by the same friend, Petya, in the woods southeast of Onega. It should be noted that a number of

Sheltozero Veps have told me that there is more "spirit activity" in this region to the southeast than in the forests around Sheltozero, where, for reasons explored in the chapter "The Bad Masters," the presence of Masters is imagined to be on the wane. Misha recounted the following:

> Those are taiga[4] stretches in the Vologidsky district—and my friend, the hunter, he does not smoke, he is a very good sportsman,[5] and this happened to him just recently. He was passing through a place in the woods where he had passed once before, 30 years ago. He had passed there when he was just a boy, 15 years old or so. He said, "So that day, I was walking, and I felt that something is looking at me.... I turned and a shadow dashes to the side, 30 or so metres from me." So he stopped walking and said, "I won't touch you, but let me leave the forest." He took a piece of bread from his satchel and put it down on a tree stump—that's what *babki*[6] teach us to do. Thirty years passed, he is going to Vatovo, and he said, "On my right, I feel something, again. So I stood still, took my gun and said, 'Yes, you see, 30 years have passed, I have gone bald and gray, and you are still here.'" Then again he took out a piece of bread, and went on his way. This was in the Vytegorskiy District.[7]

According to Misha, his friend was "marked" by the Khozyain and encountered him several more times, sometimes on hunting trips with Misha, sometimes alone. Petya, it seemed, kept finding himself in zones of active contact with the forest spirit. Another time, Misha said, Petya had bedded down for the night in a fishing hut on the shore of a lake where strange things had been happening—the kinds of rapid changes in the landscape that map onto beliefs about how Masters rearrange their domains:

> In the Vytegorskiy District, they have five lakes, interconnected, and in one of the lakes, suddenly the water disappeared; there is a funnel in the bottom, and the water, 30 metres below. And it happened virtually overnight—to a lake that is three kilometres wide and 10 kilometres long. They even sent airplanes for an aerial investigation, to try and map what happened to the water—they saw that the water levels rose, just a bit, in one of the other lakes, but other than that—nothing. So near this lake, there is this house, for fishermen, just planks to sleep on, and one bed. Petya sat down on the bed, he is sleeping, and something is choking him. He wakes up, and thinks he was dreaming, but suddenly there is creaking of the floorboards by the door. He said, "Okay, I will no longer sleep in your bed," and he went outside and made a fire and slept by the fire.

In the second instance, Petya's transgression was that he used someone else's abode without proper permission, failing to enter into a negotiation of any kind, and initially failing to acknowledge boundaries between what was his and what was not. And attention to these matters had always structured human-spirit and human-nature relations and, in that, also mirrored good relations within villages. When humans related to each other through the medium of the forest, the forest was the space where, through spatial and horticultural activities, social order within the villages was maintained as well. Nataliya, the museum director, herself from this region, explained this in her reminiscence of childhood trips to the forest with her father:

> Everyone went to their own place ... for haymaking, and where hay was prepared, there people also picked berries ... these were their places—they took care of them, trimmed excessive shrubbery, took care of their clearings, and it was all their own. Everyone had to follow the rule that when autumn came, the shrubs and the bushes have to be trimmed, as preparation for scything next year ... and then ... there wasn't like now this incomprehensible forest—meaning cut down, brought down, lying around. So, you cleaned the clearing, and—again—the wooden poles you take home, leave a few to put up the haystack later ... and the remnants of the branches that weren't useful were either burned, or stacked in a place where they wouldn't be in anyone's way—so, not in the middle of the road or a passage. And so it worked out that everyone had their own pieces of land, allocated by how the trees were maintained, and in general the forest was well maintained. And also that's how people oriented themselves—so, when you come in, you see—there are the Stryginovs' *pokosi* [cleared pieces of land]—that means, that if these are the Stryginovs' here, then the Korshunovs' pokosi follow, then our pokosi come next, then the Kokorins', and so on and so forth[8] ... and it's easy to orient yourself ... and how the reaps were spaced, sometimes it even was reflected in how people related— so, your pokosi are further away, maybe you are not as close ... but also, often to get to your reaps, you had to go through someone else's. People took care how they walked, on a designated path, and treated everyone's reaps with respect ... if there was hay lying there, people made sure to walk around it, and if a little boy or a little girl would suddenly run straight, not knowing yet, they would be punished right away—told, "You have to walk in your parents' step, you cannot walk on the hay!"

Her example here shows that the arrangements with the Master about proper behaviour and movement through the forest mirrored the importance of such propriety to good neighbourly relations and village harmony.

Beyond punishments inflicted in the forest, in Vepsian traditional ethnomedicine, improper behaviour toward natural elements (earth, fire, wind, water, and such) could also lead to physical illness, as could disrespectful treatment of the Masters. Specifically, Veps believed (and some still believe) that spitting into a fire would bring about sickness (usually chickenpox), as could spending the night in the forest under the "wrong tree" or without asking the tree's permission (the tree in question is usually a pine tree). At the same time, elements, as proxies for Masters, could also cure illnesses acquired as a result of such misbehaviour. For example, a number of illnesses could traditionally be cured by placing candles in the windows of houses standing opposite each other, the sick person's house being one of them; this practice created fire "gates" which would both "burn" the infection and quarantine it.[9]

Water was equally important for curing maladies, especially in newborns and children. For water to be used medicinally, it had to be gathered in a special way from three sources of running water, scooped in the direction of the current, and accompanied with a plea to the Master and Mistress of the Water, along with the promise to return the unused water to the same place. The incantation was a variation on the following: "'Master, Mistress, with small children! Give water, neither for guile, nor for wisdom, but for a great task—to heal [name of patient] from [name of disease].' When the water was returned, it had to be accompanied with the following thanks: 'Thank you, Master and Mistress with small children, for the water'"[10] (Semakova and Rogozina 2006, 309). If the proper protocol was not followed throughout, water would not transmit curative energy.

The Water Master (**Vodyanoy** in Russian), like the Forest Master, can reward and punish alike (while the "domestic sphere" spirits—that is, those associated with spaces and objects within the home, such as the, 309 hearth—tend by default to be more benevolently predisposed to homeowners, although they can also be angered by sloppiness, fighting, alcoholism, and other disruptive behaviours). Mirroring the rules about proper behaviour on the forest paths, there is a regimen pertaining to behaviour out on the water, when either fishing or swimming. Spitting into the water is prohibited, and throwing stones into the lake or doing household washing or laundry in the water is forbidden in the evening, in order to not disturb the Water Master's sleep; early-morning bathing is not allowed for the same reason. One of my informants told me about the game he and his friends used to play as children on the lakeshore, with one child acting as Vodyanoy, and the other children asking him for permission to swim. The "Vodyanoy" would refuse the request three times, then relent and permit swimming—"But you must not splash or fart."[11] The children would then enter the water and start splashing loudly, and imitating flatulence by blowing bubbles into the water. Then the "Vodyanoy" would try to catch the children, and the first one tagged would become the next "Vodyanoy." Although the game is irreverent, and likely appeared during general Soviet-era secularization, it does reproduce the tropes of the relationship between Veps and the water spirit: the need for permission, the clearly articulated forbidden activities, and the repercussions for disobedient behaviour. In order to curry the Water Master's favour, fishermen historically made offerings of hardboiled eggs, wine, and tobacco[12] to the water prior to setting their nets.

MASTERS AND CONTRACTS

Above and beyond the implicit contractual relationships around give and take and properly delineated behaviours, Veps historically participated in literal contracts with nature spirits. Veps cowherders, historically considered semimagical figures who were required to adhere to a number of behavioural regulations during the herding season (abstaining from sexual activity, not cutting hair, et cetera), entered into actual contracts with the forces of nature at the beginning of their herding tenure. These contracts were written on birch bark, which was then rolled up and hidden in a place known only to the cowherder. Accounts of this magical tradition vary somewhat; from various informants I have heard that each cowherder designed his own individualized contract with the Forest Master; that, because, cowherders were often illiterate, they employed the services of village sorceresses (who were often literate) to write it for them; that sometimes the text of the contract was simply a prayer (a further testament to the integration of Christian and pre-Christian religious practices); and that the birch bark was passed from one cowherder to another. But despite these variations in details, the recollections about this particular tradition always used the word *dogovor*, which would literally translate as "negotiation" but is the common Russian term for "contract." The data I gathered resonates with Russian scholarship on cowherder magic among the Veps (Azovskaya 1977; Vinokurova 2006a), including ethnohistorical accounts of the corporeality of such contracts:

> The following were the requirements of a cow-herder: the possession of the contract of otpusk [a "let"], which was purchased from a sorcerer or an old cow-herder (to learn it, the cow-herder had to go into the forest, and memorize the magical phrasing, which would then be inscribed onto the whip or the staff ... in 19th and 20th century, the handwritten version of the "let" was passed on: "In the name of the father and the son, I shall ..."; an alternative to the "let" was a direct contract with the Leshiy (forest Master), which was a less popular option because of the strict regulations it entailed.... The contract with the Leshiy was important ... according to peasant beliefs, the cows are herded not so much by the cow-herder as by the Leshiy, and thus rituals were carried out that legitimated the relationships between the village and the Leshiy, as mediated by the cow-herder. The contract with the Leshiy was entered into on day of Egoriy (April 23rd by the old calendar), or close

to Nikola day (9.05): the cow-herder, after a ritual walk-around of the herd "with crosses," and after leaving the cattle in a valley, would sit down on an aspen and call out to the Leshiy: "Tsar of forests-steppes, come here." ... "What price do you want for herding? I will give you an egg" (the egg is given to the herder on the first day of Easter). By giving the Leshiy the egg, the cow-herder secured the amplification or the renewal of the Master's force (sometimes in place of an egg animal wool was given). The contract with the Leshiy was strengthened by the requests of the owners of every cow in the herd: during the first grazing, the peasant called to the Leshiy: "Forest, tsar. Save mine ... in the field, beyond the fields, in the forest.... Here is bread and salt for you, and a bow." The Leshiy fulfilled his obligations as long as his relationship with the herders (or the cow-owners) remained intact; the herder was responsible for the actions of all of the cow-owners. (Menshenin 2000: 131)

It should be noted that the incantation features both "forest" and "tsar" as equivalents for the addressee of the request: the Khozyain. Khozyain is, in fact, the forest—the anthropomorphized incarnation of it—but such a form of address is also the recognition of the ultimate patrimonial authority, dating back to the period of Russian monarchy, when the Russian tsar was the ultimate Khozyain of the land and was commonly referred to as such throughout Russia, especially in rural contexts, as historian Orlando Figes (1997) explains. The usage of this term for authority and power continued during the Soviet period as well (as demonstrated by Rogers's example above of the Khozyain of the former state farm), and in fact, as Forrester (2006: 124) notes, current president Putin's approval ratings "seem to depend largely on voters' perception that he is a strong 'Khozyain.'"

Although cowherders (as proxies for their villages) had explicitly contractual relationships with the Forest Master, regular Veps also engaged in formalized types of exchange characterized by the articulation of offerings, obligations, and contracts. These practices persist today. While exchanges with spirits in general are an oft-described ethnographic phenomenon (Ingold 1986; Bird-David 1999) and the Vepsian practices of leaving parts of gathered berries and mushrooms for the Master on a tree stump or at a crossroads, or pouring remnants of tea onto the ground are classic forms of generalized human-spirit exchange, according to my Vepsian interlocutors, these practices are connected to contractual negotiations about the exact nature of transactions expected to take place in the forest. One informant, responding to my question "Did you address the Master when you went to the forest" and its follow-up, "What did you say to the Master?" told me that, as she had been taught by her grandparents when she was a child, upon entering the forest, she would negotiate what, exactly, she was going to take on each visit: "Master, I am coming to gather berries and mushrooms, but I won't touch any animal, I won't break any branches, I won't disturb any leaf" or "Master, I am coming for firewood, but I won't touch any animal or pick any berries."[13] I was intrigued by what seemed to me a noteworthy compartmentalization of items into subdomains of subsistence (items to gather, game to hunt, or firewood for household non-dietary needs) and tried to establish whether such distinction was common, as for me such enumeration and specificity resonated with the contractual format. Several others reported that they did not practice negotiations that classified subsistence products into separate categories, since "when you go to the forest, it's to take whatever you need," but stressed that the element of need had to be strictly adhered to through frugal and disciplined hunting or gathering; any behaviour that seemed like greed or excessive accumulation was proscribed and would be punished. This austerity approach is one common version of folklore involving the Khozyayeva of nature throughout Russian territories. In a different variation, the folklore around copper and malachite mining from the Ural Mountains, collected by Pavel Bazhov (1948) into a famous anthology, *The Malachite Casket* (which, incidentally, was read and beloved by many I met in Sheltozero), focused on luck and accumulation by those who deserve it. In this Urals lore, the Mistress (**Khozyayka**) of the Copper Mountain revealed valuable malachite deposits to impoverished serf-miners and taught them how to transform them into extravagant jewelry, which they could sell to rich customers, thereby elevating their socio-economic standing and even earning freedom from serfdom. But when greedy wealthy urban socialites tried to lay claim to the malachite jewelry without fairly compensating for it, or acquiring it through bullying or trickery, the jewelry itself would punish them by squeezing their fingers, pulling out their earlobes, and causing constant and severe bodily discomfort. These antagonists generally met bad ends in this lore, so this Mistress was also a moral regulator, who also often tested potential favourites for bravery, honestly, and fidelity, to see if their character was worthy of reward.

So to return to the questions of what a Khozyain is and what he does: in the Vepsian tradition, a Khozyain was not only the enforcer but also was himself bound by explicitly contractual negotiations and arrangements with villagers who made use of the resources of the forest. The Khozyain's capabilities were to reward and punish within the frameworks of metaphorical and literal, articulated and written contracts through actions such as sending ample game or desirable mushrooms (such as *oravgäh*, aspen mushrooms) and berries; or, through the magic of the "bad footprint," preventing a transgressor from leaving the forest, altering their perception and memory, or sending them home with an illness. The domain of the principal Khozyain of Veps was, of course, the forest (although Veps also ascribed Masters to their lakes, fields, houses, and hearths). In short, the Khozyian enforced a strict system of rules and limitations on subsistence activities, based around frugality and exchange.

MASTERS AS "FOLKLORE OF OLD DAYS"?

A question may arise: To what extent is this belief system "real" today? A skewed focus on "outdated" beliefs is a concern of many ethnographers and was a question I struggled with and engaged with over the course of my fieldwork—especially since my initial questions were straightforward queries about whether my informants themselves believed in the Masters or had had experiences with the Masters. And initially I received straightforward answers like "No, not anymore" or "No, that's what my grandmother believed." In one instance, I was told, "That stuff is for grandparents and children; we [adults] have television"—a statement holding an interesting resonance with a famous didactic Soviet cartoon called "New Year's Night" (*Novogodnyaya Noch*), which aired on Soviet television every winter holiday season and featured a competition of *chudes* (miracles, wondrous objects) between Leshiy and Ded Moroz (Grandfather Frost, the Soviet secular version of Santa Claus). Ded Moroz would consistently trump Leshiy's fairy-tale props with categorically analogous but more glamorous Soviet technology, memorably overwhelming Leshiy's "gazing plate" (a silver plate, activated by an apple rolling around its edge, that can show things happening in distant lands) with a television set.

I also based my initial assumption on conversations with Nina Zaytseva, a Vepsian scholar in Petrozavodsk, who warned me that people might feel uncomfortable with such discussions, since for much of the Soviet period, owning certain folk beliefs was constructed as rural *mrakobesye* (obscurantism). (See also Ssorin-Chaikov 2003 and Grant 1995 on the Soviet governance and "modernization" techniques that constructed indigenous peoples as being backward and traditional.)[14] The remnants of the stigma made the topic of folk beliefs as personal practice a sensitive topic for frank discussions *s chuzhimi* (with outsiders), especially since, as she noted, Veps prided themselves on being taciturn and reserved in general. Nina was speaking from experience; as her collaborator, Finnish researcher Kaja Heikkinen, wrote about their ethnographic research in Vepsian villages in the 1990s, "In the villages, people did not always understand the point of our research. Because of that, N.G. Zaytseva often had to justify our activities in one way or another. Her reply to people's puzzlement was simple and simultaneously advocating for national revival. In her opinion, Veps ought to know how they used to live.... Thus, the justification for the interviews (and in general the entire project and our presence in the village) was the strengthening of Vepsian culture" (Heikkinen 2006: 332).

As I probed further with my interview questions, I discovered that there was indeed a kind of doublespeak around the topic of the Masters that echoed Nina's comments. Veps had experienced social censure of their beliefs twice: once in the context of the aggressively atheistic Soviet discourse about nature, and more recently in the new discourses around "being modern" that came in the wake of Soviet-era rationalism (mainly in the form of increased telecommunications, and the previously inaccessible knowledge about the world at large they are supposed to provide). Consequently, Sheltozero residents were understandably reserved about discussing with strangers their personal experiences with historically stigmatized cosmologies.

But—and this was, in a way, an outcome of Nina's project, and similar research conducted in their communities—their reservations were simultaneously compounded and mediated by what they had gotten used to as typical interactions with Russian and Finnish social scientists, who still regularly visit Sheltozero and who primarily focus on historical folklore and Vepsian language revival. Now sensitized to seeing themselves through Russian and Finnish scholars' eyes as a rich repository of traditional folklore from the past, and also because Sheltozero's own native folklorist, Ryurik Lonin, had spent decades engaged in gathering folklore and material culture in a way that he explicitly framed as salvaging the past before it disappeared forever (Lonin 2000), by the time I started my project, Sheltozero Veps had come to regard the "lore of old days," explicitly framed as such, as the most valuable currency they could offer researchers.

In light of this, I, with my project about natural resources, clearly did not fit their idea of a "proper" researcher (something of which they informed me frequently), since most Russian-language research on the Veps is strictly linguistic or folklore-oriented in nature. Many of my interlocutors remained skeptical of my explanations of my research (and if they came to accept Nina's explanation of "cultural value," they did not see how either their contemporary reality or their political ecology made for a worthwhile research subject). Of course, my research agenda reflected the fact that ethnography today is far from a "salvage" operation, but the romantic mythology of "salvage ethnography," as advocated and practiced by the likes of Franz Boas and Edward Curtis, still lingered. Their ethnography was predicated on a belief that the "traditional" cultures they were studying were on the cusp of vanishing, and they had to race against time to document "authentic" Kwakiutl cultures. Clearly, many of my interlocutors in the village, in their own, matter-of-fact way and having been treated as such "salvaged" ethnographic subjects, were invested in that romantic mythology as being "the right way" to conduct ethnographic research.

This disjuncture between what my research project was and what these skeptical villagers thought it ought (or ought not) to be, was compounded by my reputation among some villagers as a scholar of "exotic" things, thanks to an interview with the public relations department of Petrozavodsk State University—my Fulbright institutional host—having gone terribly wrong. The university had a public relations department that profiled, among others, visiting international scholars. A woman who worked on the university news-paper arranged and conducted an interview with me, in which she sought to situate my research in Karelia in the context of both my life history (as a Russian-born, American-educated anthropologist) and my other fieldwork experiences. She was particularly struck by my account of an article I had just finished writing; in it, I compared the experiences of indigenous communities in the Ecuadorian Amazon and in the Cameroon rainforest with extractive and conservation industries. The subjects of the Cameroonian branch of that research project were Bagyeli people, more commonly known as pygmies. My own interviewer had many questions about my stay in Cameroon, and after I described the villages I had visited and stayed in and answered her question about the most "exotic" food I had eaten there (the answer was a tie between the delicious Safou, a.k.a. African Bush Plum, and porcupine meat), I commu-nicated what I thought were the key take-away points of my research overall: that indigenous communities around the world were often romanticized as landscape creatures that lived in perfect harmony with nature, and that those stereotypes impeded their ability to advocate for their political and economic rights and to practice self-determination, which might include participation in "modern" industries.

To my despair, the final product of our conversation was a published inter-view that misquoted me as saying that native peoples of the world were like rare flowers that we must preserve and—more saliently to my subsequent repu-tation in the village, after this interview, published on the university website, circulated back into Sheltozero—that I had lived with "wild Pygmies of Central Africa" and even went hunting with them, specifically, for porcupine. This detail came up over and over again in subsequent conversations and inter-views with the villagers, as it seemingly cemented in their heads the idea that I had somehow wandered off the correct epistemological path. More than once my interviewers would explain to me that "folklore" and "language" were the proper subjects for anthropological research, and one man—in a move that reminded me of the moment in the classic anthropological essay "Shakespeare in the Bush," in which Tiv elders patiently explain to Laura Bohannan that while *Hamlet* is a good story, she tells it wrong and should consult the elders in her own tribe to properly understand it—even recommended that I double-check with my "scientific supervisor."

All these negotiations around what knowledge I was collecting, and what was legible as "collectable" knowledge spoke to the fact that Sheltozerians did not see themselves as "exotic" or researchable, which added up to many of them essentially merely humouring me by giving interviews. But—and this is, it should be noted, a testament to the unique value of ethnographic fieldwork built on cultivating relationships that unfold and grow over time—nevertheless, after they got comfortable with me, suddenly it would be revealed, sometimes in passing, sometimes in a confessional style, that a story they had initially told about their grandmother was actually autobiographical, and that it was in fact they who had had encounters with a Master. And over time, I came to realize that their statements about the absence of Masters weren't a negation of belief in Masters, nor were they always about trying to appear "modern," as I had first assumed. The oft-repeated statements like *"Net u nas Khozyaev"* or *"Da net zdes' nikakix Khoziaev"* (We don't have Masters; There are no Masters here) reflected fairly recent cosmological adjustments triggered by the massive privatized mining and logging projects around Sheltozero and the adjoining villages. The broad impact of these projects, including on the Vepsian system of beliefs, is discussed in detail in Chapter 5.

Before we return to the Vepsian Khozyayeva, however, Chapters 3 and 4 provide the necessary background for understanding the post-Soviet changes to forests, lakes, and quarries on Vepsian lands. It is first important to understand the role that the unique landscapes of Karelia played in Vepsian lives, both in tsarist Russia and during the Soviet era. Such a resource biography of Vepsian ancestral territories is offered in the next chapter, which details how the status of the Onega lakeshore, as the first destination for health tourism in Russia, and the century-and-a-half-old mining industry in the region shaped Northern Veps' regional identity and their relationship with the political Masters in the human realm.

Notes

1. The nature of the Master was established through prefixes—*metsizand* was the precise term for the Khozyain of the forest (although as the principal spirit of this cosmology, he would often be referred to as simply *izand*); *jarvenizand* was Khozyain of the lake (sometimes also referred to as *veden izand*, Khozyain of water); *poudizand* was Khozyain of the field; *kulbet'izand* was Khozyain of the bath; and so on. Sometimes

he would be paired with a wife, the Mistress, who similarly was always *emag*, with the appropriate prefix.

2. Misha, one of my interviewees, featured later in this chapter, told me that he had encountered Khozyain as a giant black bear with red eyes, initially impervious to bullets, then appearing to bleed out, and finally vanishing suddenly, along with the blood trail. The bear was one of three, and Misha shot at them, initially thinking they were regular bears.

3. **Hondole jangele** in Vepsian; in Russian used interchangeably with "other's [*chuzhoy*] footprint" or "devil's footprint."

4. Boreal forest type, consisting primarily of coniferous tree species, associated with Siberia/the Russian North.

5. With those details, Misha conveys that his friend was of a good "moral character," contextualizing his encounters with the Master.

6. A colloquial/informal variation of *baba*, which means both "grandmother" and "old woman."

7. Approximately two and a half hours or 130 kilometres southeast of Sheltozero by car.

8. All last names of families from Sheltozero.

9. The sources for this are Semakova and Rogozina (2006), and my interviews in Sheltozero and Vekhruchey.

10. Although in general the spirit stories revolve around encounters with a single male-gendered Master, in the more comprehensive lore, the Master is sometimes envisioned as having a family.

11. Vinokurova (2006b) reports a similar game, but without the splashing aspect.

12. This contributed to the general perception of Vodyanoy as a "lesser" spirit than the Forest Master, and also a less benevolent or even neutral one—tobacco and alcohol were both "vices" Vodyanoy was believed to enjoy, while offerings to the Forest Master were generally wholesome, mostly food products.

13. Her recollection also resonates with Volkov's archival description (in Vinokurova 1989) of a Vepsian "cattle holiday" from the 1930s–1940s, marking the beginning of the grazing season. In addition to a variety of syncretic religious practices, including baking pastries and boiling eggs ("to make sure the cattle is always as round as an egg") and circling the cattle while calling upon the Apostles Peter and Paul and the Martyrs Flor and Lavr, and, finally, holding a feast, the villagers had to strictly follow the rule that forbade any kind of labour or subsistence activities until the cattle were out in the field. Volkov specifies that this ban included berry picking. "If this rule was broken, the cows of the members of the community who had transgressed, would become victims of unfortunate circumstances. As the residents told N.N. Volkov, the father of the brigade—leader F. Boytsev once after circling the cattle but before the feast already

went to work. The same day, the cow belonging to Boytsev, came back with a torn-up udder, and gave no milk that year" (1989: 124).

14. This narrative of "backwardness" has lingered on and has become, in some ways, internalized in the community. Flashes of that internationalization would sometimes become unexpectedly visible. A particularly striking example I noticed during my fieldwork had to do with the special eco-toilet that was constructed with money from a Finnish NGO. It was housed on museum land, and it was always locked. The toilet was supposed to be a pilot project, teaching Vepsian villagers how to use their waste for compost, as a part of a "modernization" and "development" program. Yet no one ever used it, and, it seemed, no one was allowed to use it. I became fascinated with this toilet and kept asking to see it; it was the only part of the entire museum complex that remained off limits to me for the first couple of months of fieldwork. Finally, I was allowed to see it (it was essentially an outhouse set up with a mechanism to facilitate the composting process), and it was explained to me that the toilet was always locked because it was actually only ever used by visitors from Moscow or St. Petersburg (or Finland); it was not for local use. When I asked why, the museum worker who showed it to me said, "You need a certain culture to be able to use it. We are village people, we don't have the right culture, not enough culture for the right hygiene."

CHAPTER 3

SPRUCE EYELASHES AND BLUE EYES OF LAKES

Museums, perhaps with the exception of the particular genre of natural history museums, are generally considered to be spaces of culture and culture-making. But, of course, the once-dichotomized relationship between culture and nature in both various ideological canons and within the discipline of anthropology itself, is increasingly seen as an artificial divide. Spatial and symbolic domains that are associated with nature and culture are enmeshed and map onto each other, metaphorically and literally. The project of what becomes designated as "nature" is cultural, and the possibilities, constraints, materialities, and even aesthetics of nature form foundations for so many aspects of "culture": subsistence practices, mythology and folklore, economies of value. While the model of the ethnographic museum that came out of Soviet emphasis on culture as a labour sector, populated by "cultural workers" in the context of broader beliefs about fundamental distinctions between humans and nature, the Sheltozero museum, by the virtue of storytelling Vepsian culture and history, makes it abundantly clear how the fates of Veps have been entangled with their natural environment through subsistence, through industry, through belief systems and practices. The museum itself is a log cabin, made of wood from Vepsian forests that, as will be shortly discussed, have served as spaces valued for their logging potential for centuries. It is located across the road from a river where, to this day, men fish and women do laundry on all but the most icy of days. As the fishermen heading to their favourite spots with their rods and bait are sometimes visible from the second-floor window of the museum, their ancestors and their tools of subsistence and trade decorate the walls of the permanent installation that meticulously documents the evolution of wooden and metal implements used in hunting and fishing in Sheltozero and surrounding areas. And the landscape surrounding the sturdy museum building during the spring and summer months—the intense green of the grass, the blue sky (sometimes coloring the river blue with its reflection), the yellow sun—are encapsulated in the flag of the short-lived Vepsian Republic on the wall of the second-floor media room. When Vepsian activists were designing a flag that would represent their identity and sovereignty, they reached for symbols that first and foremost explicitly stood for their natural environment. This environment has been historically venerated beyond the borders of Karelia; for example, in the popular Soviet song "Long Will You Dream of Karelia" that got a lot of radio play starting in 1963 and had the following lyrics:

> In different places we leave a piece of our hearts
> In our memory we treasure it carefully
> And so, now we could not help falling in love
> How could one not love this incomparable place ...
> The white night silently settled onto the cliffs
> The white night is alight, it glows
> And you cannot tell if the sky has fallen into the lake
> And you cannot tell if the lake is sailing through the sky
> And long you will dream of Karelia
> From now on
> The eyelashes of the spruce trees over the blue eyes of the lakes.

Throughout the Soviet years, the Republic of Karelia, and in particular the lake-adjacent Vepsian ancestral territories, was venerated for the beauty of its nature and cultivated as a leisure destination. It was a land of desirable resorts and sanatoriums, accessible to party officials and well-performing workers through selectively issued *putevkas* (destination permits), as well as a fertile ground for "regular" domestic nature tourism supported through an infrastructure of *turbazi* (tourist bases)—spaces dedicated to camping, basic lodging, and other tourist services. The Vepsian homeland is a landscape of coniferous forests and thousands of lakes lying east of Finland between the basins of the North and Baltic Seas, a realm of "severe northern beauty" (as the popular expression goes). It is also an abundant resource environment, with state forest stock covering over 50 per cent of the republic's territory, and 23 types of commercially valuable minerals, located by geologists, including iron ore, diamonds, vanadium, and a number of ornamental stones such as raspberry quartzite and gabbro-diabase. Other natural resources of Karelia include fresh and mineral water, as well as peat, game, fish, algae, and non-timber forest resources such as berries and mushrooms.

As was briefly discussed in Chapter 1, Veps have for centuries relied on subsistence and livelihood practices of hunting-gathering, agriculture,[1] and fishing. During the tsarist era (in this case, from the beginning of the eighteenth century, during Peter the Great's reign, until the revolution of 1917), industrial activities and resource extraction activities were added to the mix, resulting in the most common subsistence forms being swidden agriculture, fishing, and—perhaps running counter to a common imaginary of indigenous peoples "in the past"—large-scale artisanal mining and logging. As was also discussed in Chapter 1, during the Soviet era, the Veps region was a place of kolkhozes and sovkhozes (even as people maintained their forest plots), and mining and logging were managed through state programs and actors. In the post-Soviet years, there has been a return of small-scale subsistence agriculture and a dramatic acceleration of mining and logging, this time by private companies. At every point in this history, resource rights in the region have belonged to the different incarnations of the state, although currently the Republic of Karelia auctions off forest and mineral concessions to private companies, which then have virtually unlimited power throughout their concessions, as will be discussed further on.

The Veps today are concerned and anxious about both the escalation of mining and logging in the area and the rapid privatization of the lakeshore along which their villages are situated, as lakeside land is bought up by investors for luxury homes and eco-resort development.

In this chapter, I draw on the part of my fieldwork that focused on Vepsian human-nature relations beyond cosmology that pertained to their relationship to their resource-rich land, and the relationships that they formed with the various incarnations of the state through and around those abundant resources of Karelian nature. As nature tourism (in its early and later forms) developed in parallel with mining and logging, Veps came to see both as analogous ways through which they were able to exchange different aspects of "their" nature for economic and cultural benefits from the state: Karelia's climate; its "clean ecology" and its imagined curative properties, which played a large role in its popularity as a leisure destination; as well as the rare valuable minerals that have been mined since the seventeenth century. To me, as an anthropologist of human-nature relations, what was particularly interesting about the history and culture of Veps (and what consequently guided my fieldwork) was a complete lack of the commonly imagined dichotomy whereby ecotourism destinations and activities associated with nature tourism are seen as incommensurable and incompatible with extractive industries.

In academic literature, and in policy debates, extraction—as a process of separation and mobility of composite parts that make up nature—tends to be juxtaposed with activities that centre around the notion of a nature that is holistic and unparsible, as is the case with nature tourism, ecotourism, or any other activities that can be broadly grouped under the umbrella of conservation (which in Russian is usually referred to as "guarding"—guarding of nature, or guardianship of nature). Through my fieldwork, though, it became clear to me that the emphasis on physical extraction and the parsibility of the landscape, so common in discussions and debates that contrast extractive industries with ecotourism and other conservation initiatives, is not particularly meaningful from the perspective of the local Veps.

What is meaningful to them, through their lived experience, is another kind of juxtaposition: nature-based economic activities that circulate the value of their nature back into the communities versus nature-based economic activities that remove what they are entitled to from transparent and recognizable webs of exchange, leaving them disenfranchised. Veps are concerned not about extractive activities on their land per se, because for several centuries a significant component of their livelihoods has, in fact, been based on various parts of nature (minerals, wood) leaving the region or becoming physically circumscribed out of local use but remaining linked to Veps and Vepsian territories through rewarding and generative relations built with the different incarnations of the state through these natural resources. They are, rather, concerned by the erasure of those generative relations, the breaking of that link, the transformation of what might have been thought of as exportation into flat-out dispossession.

HISTORICAL ECOTOURISM IN KARELIA

"Ecotourism" is a term belonging to a particular epoch and its ideologies. As an institution, it was launched by a cluster of global governance institutions and initiatives in the 1990s. But if we think of ecotourism as leisure-oriented travel to a place where the primary attraction is nature in general, or its specific constitutive elements in particular, a prefigurative form of ecotourism has existed in Karelia for centuries: a form consistent with the Russian integration of the tourism and health sectors (Burns 1998.) At the beginning of the eighteenth century, curing illnesses with mineral waters and sea waters (thalassotherapy) was in vogue within the Russian medical paradigm. It was also a foreign form of medical intervention (Charlier and Chaineux 2009), accessible primarily to the elite, as at the time there were no healing springs in Russia, and those who could afford to do so undertook health pilgrimages to the famous healing springs of Western Europe. Tsar Peter I, as a part of his reforms in the name of modernization and improved well-being, concerned himself with locating "healing waters" within the Russian territories.

In 1714, a worker from a regional metallurgic plant discovered a healing spring source 50 kilometres from Petrozavodsk, Karelia's capital city. The worker, described as "suffering from heart illness," had been assigned to oversee the transport of iron ore. As the lore goes, the worker stumbled across the healing spring, drank from it for three days, and was fully healed. He then told the story of his magical recovery to his plant overseer, who informed the regional administrator, V. Genin, who in turn, knowing of the tsar's interest in healing springs, passed the information up the chain of command until it reached Peter I.

In 1717, Peter I deployed his personal medic to Karelia, ordering him to research the discovered springs. The water, rich in iron and other minerals, was called *martsialnaya* (martial), after Mars, the Roman god of war and iron, and appeared to be curative for anaemia, scurvy, a range of heart and liver diseases, and rheumatism (See Volfson et al.'s 2010 medical geology overview of the Russian use of minerals for curative purposes). In 1719 Tsar Peter I ordered that a health resort be constructed around the healing springs, including three wooden castles for him and his family. Peter I himself vacationed at the resort four times between 1719 and 1724. A village, named Dvortsi (Castles) and infrastructure grew around the resort, and although the high prestige of the place waned a bit after Peter's death, the interest in the healing waters continued during Soviet times. Soviet researchers launched expeditions to continue the study of water's properties in the area, and the resort was, in a sense, reborn in 1964. To this day, Dvortsi is considered a place of "clean ecology," with a sanatorium (a health-focused resort, designed to offer rest and recreation in nature) to which people from all over Russia come for health reasons.

Although in many places around the world, ecotourism or nature tourism evokes images of and the desire for "wild nature," in order to understand Russian and especially Soviet ecotourism, it is important to recognize that in the Soviet and post-Soviet conceptualization of nature and human-nature relationships, ecological tourism (whether nature tourism or ecotourism), unlike its Western counterpart, is not primarily about the experience of wilderness and "untouched" nature. The reasons for this difference lie in historical ecological and cultural politics around Russian and Soviet human-nature interactions. The manner in which the industrialization of Russia unfolded, and the demographic trends it created, ensured that there are plenty of "untouched" places within the Russian federation. Soviet economic planners believed in concentrating industries in order to maximize investment as well as production and transportation efficiency, and they successfully relocated populations as needed, in accordance with the industrial cartographies of the Soviet state. As a result, as Henry and Douhovnikoff (2008) point out, the landscape of Russia at the end of the Soviet era was, and to this day remains, a mix of environmentally degraded sites of concentrated industries, and relatively untouched areas, where local industrial development was never a part of the *gos-plan* (the government plan).

Furthermore, since for various reasons, including the institution of *dacha*[2]—country houses that functioned as vacation homes and sites of personal subsidiary agriculture for the urban proletariat (Hessler 2004; Southworth 2006)—which for generations successfully bridged the gap between urban and rural dwelling, domestic "wilderness" is not imagined to be inaccessible or exotic, even by residents of major metropolitan areas. A successful ecological tourism enterprise, then, requires added value beyond, as one of my interviewees in Petrozavodsk put it, "running from bears and wiping your butt with sorrel." In Russia, that additional value came from the strong link between ecology and ethnomedicine. Wilderness areas in general are abundant in Russia, but "healthy" wilderness is imagined to be more rare, as the national folk medical concerns produce influential cultures of formal and lay expertise that assess climatological, meteorological, mineralogical, and botanical factors that have to align for a place to meet the criteria of a "clean" or "healthy" ecology. As a result, only certain nature destinations (Karelia included) acquire reputations as sites of clean ecology and healthy leisure or even rehabilitation leisure.[3]

Thus, for historical reasons, nature tourism in Russia is associated with health and healing—physical, spiritual, and emotional. In this understanding of nature and health, Karelia's environment became renowned and sought after for its health springs and for its temperatures, which mapped onto a variety of health regimens: it was not too hot, swimming in its cold waters was beneficial for circulation, and its spruce forests were auspicious for health. In addition, an important element of Karelia's health offerings is one of its minerals, shungite: a rare black noncrystalline carbon, the largest deposits of which in the world occur in this region (local marketing flourishes, frequently representing shungite as completely unique to Karelia). Many attribute the healing properties of the aforementioned martial waters to the fact that it passes through layers of shungite, as well as to its iron content. Although heavily used in metallurgy in the 1970s, the stone is now an important part of regional ecotourism marketing, as magical healing powers are attributed to it: it is believed to have filtering or cleansing properties for water, to provide protection from "electromagnetic smog," and to preserve youth. It is fashioned into healing pyramid sculptures, massage stones, and jewelry, and it is sold in powder form as an oral health supplement.

For example, one of the sanatoriums in the Martial Waters area (Sanatorium Dvortsi), uses shungite as a draw, dedicating part of their web marketing to its medicinal qualities:

> The uniqueness of the Sanatorium Dvortsi is due to its location in a shungite-rich area where the stone reaches the open surface of the earth—this creates a microclimate

and natural state that cannot be reproduced. Shungite is the only mineral in the world that contains fullerenes[4]—the main reason for the healing powers of the stone. One of the main qualities of shungite is enrichment and deep cleansing of water. Scientists have discovered unique healing and preventative qualities of waters steeped in shungite. Shungite water has positive effects on skin: it cleanses the skin, reverses the aging process, relieves itching, heals trophic ulcers and osteomyelitis.

The sanatorium's promotional literature then goes on to describe the antihistamine qualities of shungite, as well as its "screening effect against radiation that compromises health; it weakens and slows pathological reactions triggered by electromagnetic induction of specific frequencies. Rest at the resort heals stress, headaches, and insomnia, regulates the circulatory, digestive, and cardiovascular systems, improves mental health, and increases energy and overall body tone."[5]

The sanatorium's promotional materials mobilize the "healing" history of the region, hearkening back to Peter I: "After Peter I learned about the unique antiseptic qualities of the stone, which gave the water around it great powers, Peter ordered each of his soldiers to carry a piece of shungite (though back then it was called 'aspid stone') in their hiking backpacks. Dipping the pieces of stone into pots with water, the soldiers were able to drink disinfected water."

Beyond resort marketing, there is a robust crossover medicinal/spiritual industry around shungite in the region. Some representative examples include a feature on a Woman's Day website, called "The Miraculous Qualities of Black Shungite," which, in addition to covering the scientific and apocryphal history of the Karelian stone, discusses the beliefs associated with jewelry crafted out of shungite: "It is often noted that wearing shungite jewelry concentrates energy beneficial for the body. People also manufacture protective talismans from the black stone that bring peace and thwart dark energies.... Many kinds of accessories and talismans are made from this unique black stone: pendants, bracelets, necklaces, spheres, pyramids, harmonizers, protective plates."[6]

It should be noted that shungite, while commonly marketed as the signature export of the region, is indeed commonly accepted as a healing resource by the locals. In Sheltozero, many homes (including my landlord's house) did not have indoor plumbing, and bathing took place in a *banya*, usually once or twice a week. My landlady would set up a banya for me in the way that was usual for the village: hot coals would be positioned on a large, flat shungite stone to create a "healthy energy," and water would be poured over them, releasing steam. Juniper branches aided in the process, as juniper, a plant commonly employed in herbal medicine and aromatherapy around the world, was another iconic healthy natural substance in Karelia.

Thus Karelia, especially the Vepsian region, has a long, established history as a destination for "ecological vacations," with certain locations and resources coalescing into the infrastructure of an industry: lakeside sanatoriums, "houses of leisure," healing springs destinations, pioneer camps on the lakeshore, and minerals that become both souvenirs and symbols and conduits of health, imagined to be contained in Karelian nature that was cultivated as an "ecologically clean" sector by the Soviet state. The villagers of Sheltozero fondly recollect the kind of state attention their region attracted as a state-approved and valorized place of nature, the networks of tourists returning year after year to *turbazi* around the cluster of Vepsian villages, creating both informal economic opportunities for the locals (primarily through offering lodging and food, and selling souvenirs made from local birches, as well as Vepsian traditional handicrafts) and an opportunity to interpret their nature for visitors, and demonstrate their knowledge and expertise of the region. According to my landlady in Sheltozero, Raisa, tourists solicited eagerly dispatched advice about the best berry patches, the best spots in the forest to go mushroom hunting, warnings about treacherous basins and currents on the lake, the history of the healing waters of the region, and the aforementioned magical-medicinal powers of the mineral shungite. Such sentiments stood in stark contrast to the current anxieties articulated by my Vepsian interviewees around the escalation of ecotourism, with development plans in the works for the lakeshore to become increasingly privatized and inaccessible to the local residents. As a Vepsian hunter from Sheltozero, Anatoliy, noted during an interview:

> Five years ago they took our lakeshore from us. It's a beautiful lakefront. But it is not ours any longer. *Chastniki* [private owners] have it now. First it was one company, then they resold it to another one…. Although our previous local government said we would not sell any more, some time passed, the government changed, and they auctioned it off, again…. And now no one knows what is going to happen, but like in the past this was a destination for tourists from cities, they want to build another resort like that, *na prirode* [in nature]. But this is the place for our youth to vacation, we spent all holidays there, I went swimming there all my life….
>
> Did you see that the river enters the lake? When the wind is from the lake, the water is warm in the lake, everyone swims there … when the wind comes from the shore, everyone goes swimming in the river. When it was hot in the summers, everyone would go there, it was such a good respite from the heat. And this was all sold into private hands, that means, now there will be fences, because we are … well … we are not very cultured, we always leave trash after ourselves. What is there to say … of course, *chastniki* are not going to clean up after us, and we lost the lakeshore. And if this was really ours, we could decide we are not going to give it up. But now we have no say, it will be all for tourists who come to be in nature.

Nina, the director of the Sheltozero department of forestry, which was an important location for data collection during my fieldwork, confirmed that, although such practices are not yet large scale in the region, new forest and water regulations make such a threat more real. Already in Podmoskovye (the rural region in the vicinity of Moscow), she said, "They do rent out lakes or part of lakes, and then no one local can get in—it is a real thing. If the law allows it, and it does, it is a real thing." And, as her colleague Sasha at the department of forestry notes, even if tourism companies are not motivated to provide access infrastructure in terms of roads, the mining and logging industry in the area is taking care of just that. And both of them confirm that, essentially, anyone with the money and inclination can buy and sell parts of the lakefront that is reputed, historically, to be full of healthy water, sometimes locally called "live water." Interestingly, this discourse fuses ethnohydrological and ethnomedical discourses of the bioavailability of certain "healthy" minerals and energies in water (the idea that water can carry healing energetic charges) with the Russian fairy-tale trope of "live water," which, in storybooks, has the power to heal, rejuvenate, and even bring the dead back to life. "Live water" is juxtaposed with "dead water" in both fairy tales (where the latter can kill) and common usage; in Sheltozero, and, in fact, in much of rural Russia, both bottled water and boiled tap water are imagined to be "dead water." Although the common usage of "dead water" is more prosaic and less dramatic than its fairy-tale counterpart, these ways of talking about water are ethnographically important, because they point to anxieties about the annexation of lakes and lakefront territories being experienced as more than simply the transfer of property—a diversion of literal and metaphoric currents of health that have animated the local imaginary of the residents in their history of themselves and their region.

As Nina and her co-worker explain, land investment and land speculation along the lakefront is easy. The only requirement is that a company with business interests in the lakefront be established; the company can then be sold. "You can't just sell the lakefront, so you have to create a company, and then you can sell the company together with the lakefront—but the company can be fictitious," I was told.

ELITE MINERALS OF THE VEPS REGION

Karelia is famous not only for its aforementioned and commemorated in song "spruce eyelashes" and its clean ecology, but also for massive deposits of dimension stone: natural rock material that is extracted from quarries with the goal of producing slabs of varying shapes and sizes. While the most common dimension stones are granite, marble, limestone, and the like, the chain of

Vepsian villages along the western shore of Lake Onega is the site of two rare minerals (besides shungite, which is not a dimension stone): raspberry quartzite and gabbro-diabase. The heart of this local extraction zone is the village of Rybreka, the village of Shoksha, and the industry town of Quartzitniy, which adjoins Shoksha. Rybreka is the next village up the road from Sheltozero, and many Sheltozero men work at the stone quarries around Rybreka. Shoksha and Quartzitniy are located next to quarries of the rare ornamental stone that, in a literal translation from Russian, is called raspberry quartzite but, in the English-language literature about it, is more often referred to as crimson quartzite or purple porphyry. This quartzite is sparse, since Karelia is the only place in the world where it is commercially mined. (Though structurally analogous, similar types of quartzite are found elsewhere in the world.) In fact, sometimes the stone is eponymously simply called shoksha, after the place where it is found.

Immediately adjoining Rybreka is a sequence of quarries where gabbro-diabase, another dimension stone used for memorial stones and in road construction, is extracted. Although less rare than raspberry quartzite, gabbro-diabase is found in commercial quantities in only three places in the world: Australia, Ukraine, and Karelia. In this section I show, through a historical overview of the particular cultural and political dynamics that emerged around the mining of these two rare minerals, that for the Veps, mining generated spheres of exchange that linked the procured stone with significant economic capital and extraordinary cultural capital and prestige, in some

Figure 3.1 Pieces of raspberry quartzite at the museum

sense analogous to the cultural and economic benefits generated by the status of Karelia as a cultivated elite ecological destination.

Raspberry quartzite has been mined in the region since the middle of the eighteenth century, although today only a crushed stone quarry for shoksha remains active. Raspberry quartzite was often called the tsar's stone. It was an elite cosmopolitan mineral destined for the construction and decoration of royal landmarks and high-profile buildings; most notably, Tsar Nicholas I gifted raspberry quartzite to France, a slab of stone that would be fashioned into Napoleon's sarcophagus (hence the photograph of it in the village museum). In 1859, a monument to Nicholas I himself was erected in St. Petersburg, also made out of raspberry quartzite. In addition, the stone had a transnational dimension, as it seemed to enchant foreign architects and designers—a marker of prestige in Russia, which had long experienced an ambivalently aspirational relationship with the West. In the 1770s, Italian architect Antonio Rinaldi used it for the foundation of the Chesme Column, a monument erected in Tsarskoye Selo to commemorate Russian naval victories in the Russo-Turkish War. Several years later, Charles Cameron, the neoclassical Scottish architect to Catherine the Great, used it to decorate the interior of the royal summer residence, also in Tsarskoye Selo. French-born Auguste de Montferrand, in the service of Alexander I, designed what would become the chief Russian Orthodox church, St. Isaac's Cathedral in St. Petersburg, and decorated the steps leading up to the altar with raspberry quartzite.

Onega Veps were renowned for their mastery of raspberry quartzite, and stoneworkers' brigades regularly accompanied the mineral to elite construction sites in major metropolitan areas, so cultural capital was part of the established regime of exchange around this mineral. Many families in the village have family lore from grandfathers and great-grandfathers who were involved in this form of labour. In fact, the Veps ethnographic museum in the village of Sheltozero has a wall dedicated to these brigades.

The display stresses the cultural capital associated with mining in the region. Visitors are familiarized with the concept of othodnichestvo (a feudal-era term meaning temporary labour migration, discussed in Chapter 1), with the display text noting that while village men pursued various types of work (including agricultural, construction, and furnace work), "stoneworker Veps received particular glory." The display text adds, "The extraction and processing of raspberry quartzite demanded skills and knowledge that were passed from generation to generation over the course of centuries. Thus arose entire dynasties of stonemasters." Also featured is a photograph of a stoneworker brigade from Sheltozero on a construction site in St. Petersburg and a photograph of Napoleon's sarcophagus, made from Tsar Nicholas I's aforementioned gift to France. The Sheltozero Veps feel that the honour of this gift links their little village to an event of historical proportions in the global arena (and a much larger photograph of Napoleon's sarcophagus is prominently displayed in the community room of the museum). The stoneworkers did not accompany the purple stone to Paris, but they travelled to other metropolitan areas, bringing the prestige and cachet of city culture back to the village in the form of souvenirs and stories, treasured alike. "The money was good," said one of the museum workers to me, as we were looking at the display together, "and when they came back, the stories [about their travels] were good, too."

The stone's elite status carried over to the Soviet era, when it was used exclusively for the Communist Party and government needs, and Sheltozero and the Vepsian miners continued to be linked through the stone that only they could deliver to the Soviet seat of power and the various objects that represented and venerated it. Raspberry quartzite was most famously used in the construction of Lenin's mausoleum, where it was used as a part of the top pyramid, and the walls of the repository; the word "LENIN" was encrusted in raspberry quartzite against the backdrop of black labradorite. As Irina, an older woman from the village recalled about a trip with the Veps National Choir to Moscow in the 1980s: "They took us on an excursion, and finally we come to the mausoleum, and there it is: the word, the name, Lenin, and imagine that, the stone came from our village, procured with our men's hands." On a local level, the Petrozavodsk bronze statue of Marx and Engels, unveiled in 1960 and designed to commemorate the 40th anniversary of the Karelian Labour Commune, boasts a base of raspberry quartzite.

In an overlapping timeline, the production of gabbro-diabase, in the quarries farther down the lakeshore, escalated during the Soviet years. Under Soviet authority, there was a single gabbro-diabase quarry that, like the raspberry quartzite quarry, was managed by an administrative office responsible for all minerals in the region. Gabbro-diabase, while less ostentatiously luxurious than raspberry quartzite, was a part of Soviet state-building and infrastructure-building projects. The first gabbro-diabase quarries opened in 1924, after the stone was assessed by early Soviet geologists as being optimal for road construction due to its density and resistance to extreme temperatures. The initial mining project used approximately 600 workers; as one of the quarry administrators, who is also a local history buff, told me in an on-site interview,

> In Rybreka and around, there simply weren't that many people to do extraction ... so then it was decided to bring people here, to Rybreka ... barracks were built for the men, and, understandably, a year later, new families began to form in Rybreka.

But where to put the little children? Nowhere! Because they didn't have their grand-mothers here. So, in 1926 a childcare of sorts was built ... which then was trans-formed into a proper kindergarten. Then the issue was—people live here, they get sick ... and then in Sheltozero, in 1928, the first hospital was built ... so, the devel-opment of industry brought kindergartens and hospitals.

In addition to Karelian Veps' land becoming the point of origin for the circu-lation of luxurious raspberry quartzite and sturdy, practical gabbro-diabase, the wood from its forests has historically been a source of Vepsian pride. Although the elite nature of Karelian woods seems to be more apocryphal or at least less documented than the stories of the dimension stones—possibly because the wood is more anonymous and somewhat more ephemeral than a very rare decorative stone—local narratives recount that in the eighteenth century, their woods were especially commissioned for and used by the royal navy, narratively establishing yet another link between the Veps and the ultimate authority in the Russian land: the tsar, Peter the Great, who was not only foundational to the establishment of the region as a leisure destination but also the tsar referenced in the common term for royal raspberry quartzite, tsar's stone. It is easy to see how the materi-ality of Vepsian nature not only drew profit and respect into the area's commu-nities but also became a part of Veps' mythology and narrative of themselves as skilled workers, as rural people who, through the uniqueness of their natural resources and their skill with them, transcended the common association—which persisted in Russia through the tsarist years and the Soviet years alike—of rural-ness with backwardness. The next chapter, though, shows how these human-nature relations have played out since the collapse of the Soviet Union, and the ruptures that emerged in what had historically been the fabric of connectivity between Veps and the various incarnations and scales of the state.

Notes

1. Although the agricultural context in Karelia is very different from what is generally represented as "rural Russia" in agrarian studies, as those tend to focus on central Russia with its *chernozem* (black earth), and is removed from the stereotypes of Russia as a fertile breadbasket of Europe. Although Karelia followed the national arc of agrarian collectivization and decollectivization in terms of the social and economic restructuring of the region, and is a part of the agrarian political ecology of the Soviet Union and Russia, subsistence agriculture means very different livelihoods in Karelia and other "Boreal North" regions than it does in more southern regions.

2. As Southworth (2006) notes, although the term "dacha" historically referred to the summer retreats of the nobility or Soviet elites, it has come to be a catch-all term

for any sort of garden house, from a suburban mansion (often called *kottedzh* to evoke the British "cottage") to a plot of land with a shack made of scrap wood.

3. A cursory look at promotional materials for various eco-destinations would reveal the factors used in formulating an assessment of a place as having a clean ecology: clean rivers linked to healthy leisure; the curative properties of nature; "soft winter and stable summer good for the blood pressure"; and health-supporting forest scents, in particular coniferous ones, but also cedar groves, et cetera.

4. Fullerenes, "discovered in 1985 by researchers at Rice University, are a family of carbon allotropes named after Buckminster Fuller. They are molecules composed entirely of carbon, in the form of a hollow sphere, ellipsoid, or tube" (https://www.sciencedaily.com/terms/fullerene.htm, accessed August 1, 2016).

5. From http://dvortcy.ru/about/lechebnye_faktory/shungit/, accessed on August 5, 2016 (my translation).

6. From http://www.wday.ru/krasota-zdorovie/sok/chudodeystvennyie-svoystva-chernogo-shungita/, accessed August 16, 2016.

CHAPTER 4

THE BAD MASTERS

On the wall of the rustic, wooden building that houses the Veps ethnographic museum, there is a prominent photograph, gifted to the museum by visiting French photographer Georges Azra, of Napoleon's already mentioned sarcophagus in the Église du Dome in Paris. During my first visit to the museum, as I was settling into Sheltozero, one of the museum workers, Lyudmila, glanced at it, sighing, "We used to be famous for this stone, and for our skills with this stone. And the stone went to famous places. And now we don't know where they take the stones, but they take them day and night, on giant trucks, all the roads are broken, and we don't even have the money to repair the kindergarten." "*Nu eto pravil'no?*" she added, which in literal translation means "Is it correct?" although the actual meaning is closer to "Is it fair?"

The last decade has seen a dramatic escalation in extractive activities in the region, as well as a fundamental restructuring of the actors and governance parameters involved. The new Russian Forest Code, adopted in 2006, promoted decentralization and market liberalization in forest management, a sector that is responsible for mining concessions, as they are located inside the forests and are often conjoined with logging enterprises. As a result, while privatization is facilitated in a fashion that allows the state to accumulate wealth and consolidate power, on the regional level, state-run enterprises have given way to multiple private enterprises that are generally incorporated outside the Republic of Karelia and thus are not taxed as corporate entities with the republic. While the republic's government generates wealth for itself (and for the federal treasury) through the hefty concession fees the companies pay on republic-level auctions, the companies do not invest anything into the local economies. With the exception of the low-wage, dangerous manual labour opportunities they provide for the local men, the companies neither undertake nor fulfil any financial obligations to the locals.

While production of raspberry quartzite, which brought glory and material capital to the region for a long time, as discussed in the previous chapter, is on the wane, the gabbro-diabase business is booming. Where previously there was one centralized state-run office, staffed by locals, overseeing the extraction of both regional minerals, there is now a fluctuating number of gabbro-diabase quarries run by private companies, some of them foreign or involving foreign partners.

In my interviews with the Veps in Sheltozero and the nearby "mining village" Rybreka, many informants articulated discontent over and anxieties about the expansion of the mining companies. They were seen as decimating, and putting physical barriers around, previously publicly accessible sectors of the forest, creating no-passage zones, with very few limitations, as the Russian Forest Code largely disempowered local forestry departments and instead empowered private companies to manage their own forest concessions. Both logging and mining companies bid for "forest rental" (*arenda lesa*) concessions, and thus their provenance now includes many activities previously managed by state-run forestry departments.

In fact, the escalation of mining is connected with the escalation of logging, as mining activities are often combined with logging activities through the empowerment of multi-purpose companies referred to as "megarenters." Such companies sign contracts for forest concessions that they can use for logging or mining, interchangeably or simultaneously. As the previously separately administered industries of mining and logging are now conjoined through the commercial privatization of space, in place of a state-run program managing both strictly regimented logging and the replanting of the forest through the department of forestry, there are now private logging companies, many subcontracted by Finnish operators, right across the border. In my interviews with the Veps in the villages of Sheltozero and Rybreka, many informants—including the miners who, on their daily commutes, witness the forest receding—articulated discontent and anxieties about the forest being rapidly cut down and being taken away ("Across the border day and night, day and night, the trucks go"): the opposite of the historical memory of the highly regimented logging of regional woods, destined for the tsar's own navy.

The Veps complain about this turn of events, the indiscriminate logging, and the ever-expanding mining, with organic and inorganic resources literally extracted from the region on large trucks with unclear destinations, most clearly articulated as za granitsu, which means "across the border" or "beyond the boundary." When I asked one Sheltozero resident which border was meant, he waved his hand in an indeterminate direction, "Ah, all of the borders. With Finland, and the border of the republic, and the border of the okrug.

And past the border. Well, no one knows where they go, really." This anxiety about the unknown space "across the border," where the regional resources enter commodity chains that are not recognizable or comprehensible to the locals, paralleled local narratives about the transition between past transparency and the present anonymity of economic webs connecting the Veps, the resources from their territories, and resource brokers and consumers. As one interviewee, whose father and grandfather had worked in the mining sector, put it, "Back then [during the Soviet years] there was one big quarry, we knew exactly who was running it, and they had to report to us ... and they did: once a month we had a gathering. Now nobody knows even who owns the quarries. [It's a] commercial secret, you see!"

Of course, nostalgia in such references to the "good old Soviet times" must be engaged critically. Certainly, Veps villages, like many others, experienced tensions with the Soviet state, especially during collectivization, and ethnographic interview details suggest that nostalgia for Soviet times is really primarily nostalgia for the relatively stable period from 1970s onward. Nonetheless, it is also necessary to understand the importance of the long-term history of Vepsian cultural capital in the realm of stoneworker skills, as understood by Veps themselves: it is their mythology of their past that in a sense served as the foundation for a stable sector of the economy for many years. But especially in the field of post-Soviet studies, the subject of "nostalgia" has long been a somewhat misleading in its focus on, as Oushakine (2007: 452) put it, "the illusory aspect of the current longing for the glorious socialist past, which may or may not have existed." I contend that, in this case, dismissing positive recollections of the past as a mere nostalgic construction is misleading, for several reasons: First of all, as Oushakine suggests, "antinostalgia" criticism tends to overlook the function of enframing discourses in nostalgia, whereby evocations of "old" forms are a commentary on the inability of existing or new symbolic forms to communicate relevant content; this certainly seems applicable in the case of the Veps, whose narratives of the past not only recount now-defunct social relations but also comment on the barrenness of new, non-generative social relationships with the new set of Masters. Second—although I am cautious to not reproduce the reified before/after dichotomy so common in narratives of postsocialism, especially since the story of Veps and their natural resources precedes the Soviet years—it is relevant that for the Veps, the tsarist-to-Soviet transition was a narrative of continuity and renegotiation, while the Soviet-to-post-Soviet transition has been a narrative of rupture.

So, during my fieldwork, I wrote down an oft-repeated story, significant in Sheltozero's lore, of a raspberry quartzite stoneworker brigade, away on one of their prestigious deployments, becoming trapped in Petrograd[1] without passports during the 1917 revolution, but successfully establishing their expertise and relevance with the authorities who detained them, and returning home before going on to become valued Soviet stoneworkers. On the symbolic level, the story is about effectively renegotiating the social contract with the brand-new Soviet state, and it stands in stark contrast to post-1991 narratives of deskilling and diffusion of accountability within the regional extractive industries. And whatever perspective one takes on the role of nostalgia in the post-Soviet milieu, a historical look at the political economy of extraction in the region supports at least the mining-focused aspect of the Veps' narratives of "good old times"; both before and after the revolution, mining provided a respected and well-compensated occupation and generated an influx of goods, services, and cultural capital.

The previous chapter provided an overview of Karelian natural "treasures" and the way in which Vepsian livelihoods and even personhoods have been linked to their resources. As I have already outlined, for Veps, historically nature has been both the medium and the object of social transactions: the medium of their relationship with the Master of the Forest, and the space where certain kinds of social rules and expectations about relationships between neighbours and neighbouring villages are played out (Nataliya's reminiscences about the strict spatial organization of pokosi in the forests, discussed in Chapter 2, is one example). It is also the medium and the object of transactions with a succession of greater Masters: the tsars, the Soviet authorities, and now the new entrepreneurs, who have dramatically escalated the long-established and, from the Veps' perspective, reasonably paced logging and extraction processes.

Once the medium of exchange itself is radically transformed—quarries expanded, forests cut down at a drastic speed—and the practices of exchange radically altered on all scales, the supernatural beings charged, in the Vepsian cosmology, with maintaining the regulatory framework that ensures fair exchange have a new place (or no place) in these profoundly altered physical and metaphysical spaces. And, indeed, from the early days of my fieldwork, when I interviewed people in Sheltozero and neighbouring villages about the cosmology of the Masters, the stories, whether offered up as folklore or personal experiences, were often accompanied by comments like "We don't have Masters anymore." At first I interpreted such statements as an indicator of a gradual waning of traditional spiritual beliefs. But, as often happens— and ought to happen—in the ethnographic process, as I spent more time in the field and dug deeper, my initial assumptions were proven wrong.

My first inkling that I was misinterpreting such statements came while I was watching television with my host family, a Veps fireman and his wife, and their visiting relatives. *Tul'skiy-Tokarev*, the miniseries about a serial killer in 1970s Leningrad we watched every night, had just ended, and my landlord was channel-surfing, then settled on what appeared to be a procedural (the name of which I never found out), which that evening dealt with a legal team from the office of prosecutor of the republic investigating illegal logging in Karelia. The legal investigators marched to the office of the building contractor's company and, clearly the "good guys," courageously stood their ground until the company supervisor allowed them to compare the legally specified borders of the concessions with the location of the suspected illegal activities. We all watched, enthralled. "That would never happen," commented one of the visiting relatives during a commercial break. "Really? Why not?" I asked. "Because they never let anyone do inspections," he said, adding, "There is no accountability, and no punishment; they just do what they want." I joked, "Maybe the Masters will punish them and put them on a bad footprint." To this he replied, "What Masters? We don't have the Masters anymore—where are they going to live? All the forest is gone. No forest, no Masters."

How Veps conceptualize the Masters' mobility is something I was interested in from the get-go. My questions about how and whether the Masters can move around in space had yielded illustrative stories of how, in the past, Khozyayeva could relocate (from a particular hearth or a hunting shack, a particular lake, or a particular part of a forest), stressing their ability to do that, rather than where they would then go, replying *"Kuda zaxotyat, tuda i uydut"* (They will go wherever they want) and *"Raz ushli—znachit, vse"* (Once they have gone, then that's it), but at first I failed to interpret their absence as departure, not non-existence. At first I had reached for a conventional anthropological interpretive script in analysing my interviews, supposing that processes of modernization were weakening and erasing the beliefs in these nature spirits, but as it turned out, that script was insufficient. The Vepsian cosmology of Masters had always linked cosmological and political worlds—worlds structured through contractual relations with different kinds of Masters—and in this post-Soviet, privatized economic space, it had not ceased to do so. In other words, the claims of "no Masters" I was transcribing from my interview recordings were more complicated than a straightforward disavowal of the cosmology in question.

I had already been interviewing villagers about the changes in their forest and knew that in the last decade it had been transformed by the aggressive logging of private contractors, with the wood going across the border to Finland under cover of night, debris left behind. Complaints about this turn of events stood in stark contrast to narratives about tsarist-era selective removal of trees destined for the royal navy, and strictly regimented Soviet-era logging, when forest replanting was closely monitored, largely because (as expounded upon in the previous chapter) during the Soviet era Karelia was cultivated as a leisure destination, a land of desirable sanatoriums accessible to party officials and well-performing workers through selectively issued *putevki* (destination permits). The logging companies of today not only fail to replant, but in fact impede forest regrowth by leaving behind sectors of cut-down forest, the forest floor barely visible through the tangles of dead branches and strewn debris, and looking, according to Nataliya, "as if after a war. Like we were bombed."

In light of these stories about the forest, the comment made by my landlord's relative made me reconsider the previous answers about people no longer believing in Masters that I had diligently recorded. I had been interpreting them as a conscious distancing from traditional narratives for reasons of self-consciousness about not being "modern." I was able to follow up explicitly with six of the individuals with whom I had done topical interviews up till that point, this time specifically asking them to elaborate on folk beliefs about the Masters.[2] While one of them reaffirmed his previous statement that Master lore was "all grandmother's tales," the rest, when prompted by me a second time, gave elaborations that departed from the "grandmother's tales" interpretation. Their second-round responses ranged from "It is hard to believe the Masters are there when the forest is so different" to "What they did to the forest ... how can any spirit remain there now?" to "If the Masters were still there, they wouldn't allow *vse eto* (all this)"—said while pointing to a stretching pile of refuse near the quarries).

BAD CONTRACTS AND BAD MASTERS

"All this," according to interviewees, also includes lack of investment by the new mining companies into the local economy. With the exception of the low-wage, dangerous manual labour they provide for the local men, the companies neither undertake nor fulfil any financial obligations to the locals. They are incorporated outside of Karelia and thus are not taxed as corporate entities within the republic; the concession fees they pay are not locally redistributed. This makes people vocally bitter, since local management and financial administration of mineral resources were two of the goals of establishing the aforementioned short-lived administrative Volost'—and most believe that it was precisely this issue of mineral wealth that led to the forced dissolution of the Volost'.

"They have all these quarries for stone, which, as far as I know, is valuable; it costs quite a bit of money. But if there were any profits from it allocated to the local budget, then maybe [the village administration] wouldn't live so poorly, wouldn't sit in that old hut of a kindergarten near the school—they could build themselves a normal building, at least with running water," says

Nina to one of her co-workers at the *Lesnichestvo* [department of forestry], one of my participant-observation sites in the village. Nina, as the supervisor, is in charge of concessions paperwork—although that means something very different now than it did prior to the implementation of the new Russian Forest Code, with its decentralization and market liberalization in forest management. "They don't invest locally; they are megarenters," snorts the co-worker derisively.

Nina explains, "A forest sector can be rented with different goals: can be rented for logging, or can be rented for mineral extraction. So, the megarenter we had, who owned the logging company, he is gone now—and the megarenters from the quarries, they are still here. There are a lot of them." Nina's comment about the lack of investment in the local economy echoes routine complaints by every person I interviewed or had informal conversations with during the course of my fieldwork. The forest is being cut down, the wood is being taken away, and the mining companies are expanding, alternately decimating and putting physical barriers around previously publicly accessible sectors of the forest, creating no-passage zones. As the villagers see it, the physical habitat of the Masters is being removed in the context of this new economy that, from Veps' perspective, is anything but moral. And compounding that is the fact that according to the new forestry regulations, as Nina and her co-workers explain, the quarry owners are what are locally called "megarenters"[3]: large companies that receive concessions for territories from the state (through the department of forestry) with very few limitations. In fact, they are even supposed to assume some of the previous functions of the forestry departments, such as putting out fires (the forestry department was particularly outraged by this development, and Nina's partner told me about having to hide "behind some bushes" to fight fire with equipment they had to lie about no longer having). So while the concessions for the quarries are actually "forest rentals" of a specific territory with the goal of mineral extraction, within that territory they have almost total control of the forest; therefore, when they need to cut down parts of the forest in order to expand the quarries, they are legally empowered to do so.

Thus, in a very literal sense, the megarenters, the new Masters of the quarries, are now the Masters of the forest, as it is now part of their legal purview. They have both supplanted and displaced older agencies of the state, such as the forestry department, which now has to ask permission (and can be denied) to do any inspection—hence my landlord's relatives' knowing and cynical disbelief about the fictional portrayal of that process on the TV procedural—and they have been systematically physically decimating the habitat of the spirit Masters.

THE END OF PROPER EXCHANGE

As noted in Chapter 2, the Vepsian belief system was predicated on proper or fair exchange with the Forest Masters, pertaining to and enacted within the medium of nature, and historically mediated through strict cosmological contracts. The contracts with the state (both tsarist and Soviet) mirrored the spirit contracts in the sense that both states offered regulation and exploitation frameworks pertaining both to nature and to Veps' general well-being. Nature was exchanged in a way that the Veps perceived to be fair and within limits, and nature also became the medium where the social contract between Veps and the state was made manifest. The labour that went into preparing ship-building wood or extracting raspberry quartzite was rewarded both monetarily and with status, and during the Soviet regime, these exchanges of/through local nature triggered welcome benefits of the social contract with the state, with hospitals, kindergartens, and schools arriving to service the quarry workers who serviced the state. All of these exchanges were, above all else, understood and verbalized in ways centreing on notions of fairness and appropriateness: "In the past, things were the way they should be,"[4] "That was the right way; we worked for the state, and the state provided us these benefits," "We gave a part of our land, of ourselves, but back then everyone knew and respected Veps stone masters—and when they came back, the money was good."[5] In other words, the way in which the flow of labour, goods, and services between the different actors was regulated formed a moral economy framework, which found symbolic expression in the narrative of the Masters. Conversely, the Masters were charged with ensuring its continued balance and fairness.

An important aspect of this anxiety about space—a space so alienating to Veps that their Masters cannot inhabit it any longer—has to do with the concept of borders. For one, as I gleaned from interviews, mining and logging companies were seen to decimate and put physical barriers around previously publicly accessible sectors of the forest, creating no-passage zones, with very few limitations, for the reasons explained earlier in the chapter—the fact that the Russian Forest Code largely disempowered local forestry departments and instead empowered private companies to manage their own forest concessions in their capacity as megarenters. This management of space and resources, scrambling previously established economic and moral infrastructures around them, has generated anxiety in local residents. The complaint mentioned earlier in this chapter—[It's a] commercial secret, you see!"—exemplifies that anxiety, as does Lyudmila's comment, quoted at the opening of this chapter, about the "famous" stone being taken away to unknown places.

An echo of this preoccupation with resources disappearing beyond borders came up in an interview I conducted with Anatoliy Pavlovich, the president of the Sheltozero hunters' association. I originally planned to interview him, in life-history format, about his impressions of the transformations in the mining and logging sectors, but he ended up talking primarily about wild game, another natural resources for which rural Karelia is famous. Pavlovich spent a large part of our interview engaging in the kind of before-and-after comparison that characterized a lot of the discourse in Sheltozero about the changes that took effect during the post-Soviet era. "Look," he told me,

> In the old times, when I was just joining [the association] as a member ... I joined the Hunters' Association in the 1970s. I gave my friend, who was going to Petrozavodsk, three rubles for the membership dues, he got me the ticket—and that's it! I could go hunting. Open season would start, and there I would be, out in the forest. For example, we hunted moose. What would often happen is this: I would kill a moose, take the meat to the store, and get a percentage of the sale price for the meat. So it's a job, in a sense, not just subsistence. I also had sports licences, like for hunting bears. Then the moose stopped being a general licence target and became a sports licence animal—then it would cost fifty rubles to kill a moose. It's both a lot of money and not that much.... Then they allowed us to kill moose in exchange for killing two wolves: you catch and destroy two wolves, you get a moose. And today ... if I go today, if I come across a bear and kill it, and someone sees me with this bear—that's it, that is poaching. I would lose the hunting licence, the hunting rifle....

I asked him about the history of restrictions on the wildlife, and he explained the escalation in pricing, connecting it, angrily, with the new practice of "saving" and "delivering" wild animals for "foreigners." When I asked him what he meant, he explained: "Here, on our side [of the border], you know, it's cheaper. So the Finns come, to the places where there is abundant wildlife, bears, wild boars—they shoot them and they pay, they pay a lot. For us eight hundred rubles is a lot, and for them, eight hundred euros is not a lot, it's a reasonable price. Maybe even more now, I am not sure." When I asked why there was such a disparity in prices, he said,

> Well, the pricing is different for them. And the Hunters Association, they mark up the price, they create a tier for the foreigners, and they invite them—really for their own financial survival, but under the guise of exchange of best hunting practices, et cetera. And on their side, better believe you me, it is very different. I was driving through Finland and I saw—they have roe deer, just running around, across the road. No animals run around like that here; here they are shot, poached. The Finns, they have very strict laws, they don't hunt their nature, but they can come across

the border and pay a lot of money, and hunt our animals. But so they can hunt our animals, we are now barred from doing what we have always done.

In general, the juxtaposition of how things "used to be" with how they are at present was a common leitmotif in my interviews with the Veps, one which poses an interesting and important ethnographic problem. On the one hand, it would not benefit the ethnographic goal to uncritically accept and reproduce overtly nostalgic narratives of "good old Soviet times." Certainly, Veps villages, like many others, experienced tensions with the Soviet state, especially during the process of collectivization and relocation, as is discussed at length in Chapter 1. But at the same time, in some contexts and for some groups, the rupture created by the fall of socialism may be central to the experience of livelihood. A historical look at the political economy of resource extraction in the region at least partially supports the nostalgia of the Veps' narratives of the past, especially in comparison with their situation today, when they have less and less agency and compensation in the extractive industries even as the nature around them is being monetized more and more in various ways. Both before and after the revolution, mining provided a respected and well-compensated occupation and generated an influx of goods, services, and cultural capital. Veps in the past were involved in the bureaucracy and governance of the mines and the forest sectors as state workers, and they took pride in this work; currently, their primary participation in these industries is as under-compensated manual labourers, working in unsafe conditions. My interviewees complained about lack of safety equipment, the cutting of meals for workers on shift, and indifferent, mocking managers, among others.

One day, while I was pondering this issue of dislocated/disappearing Masters, I interviewed Oleg, a miner working in the quarry owned by a company from Kazakhstan, who told me, "We no longer have Khozyayeva [pronounced with the regular stress on the second syllable of the Russian word]; the new ones we have now, we now have Khozyayeva [the same word, but pronounced with the stress on the fourth syllable]." Oleg performed a word-internal modification—a lexical stress shift, a linguistic phenomenon that I, as a native speaker, recognized was used to communicate derision— a denotative move somewhat analogous to putting something in air quotes. The non-standard pronunciation was used to negatively evoke the stereotypical "new Russian" dialect. In the symbolic universe of post-Soviet Russia, the new Russians are associated with excessive wealth, accumulated through violent, corrupt means, and known for placing themselves above any law or moral code (Patico 2000). Indeed, when I asked, "Why do you call them

Khozyayeva?" (mimicking his stress shift), he replied, "We [the miners] call them that because they do whatever they want; it is total bezpredel."

The ecological and economic practices of logging megarenters, who had already cut down large parts of the forest, and of the quarry owners, who literally governed the remaining forest, underlay statements made by my informants, such as "There is no forest anymore, so there are no Masters" and the juxtaposition by Oleg and other miners of the old Masters and the new, lexically differentiated, unfair masters. "*Plokhie oni, plokhie Khozyayeva*" (They are bad, bad masters), said Oleg later, when discussing the quarry owners mocking of the workers' request for a raise during the unprecedented heatwave that had killed thousands of people across Russia in 2010. "They said, 'Why do you need a raise? Look at the suntan you got, like vacationing in the South'"—referring to vacation destinations on the Black Sea popular in Soviet times and today.

FROM MASTERS AND CONTRACTS TO "BEZPREDEL"

The elite natural resources of their land have served for Veps as the medium of connection to the powers that be, through layers of exchange: local resources for state benefits and skilled labour for economic and cultural capital. Economies organized around the central figures of the tsar, and later the Soviet state, ensured an exchange system in which participants were known and visible, trade routes were clearly defined, and expectations were managed and met. Those same expectations—of prosperity, of prestige—are now disappointed and disordered. Veps' nostalgia about the "good old days of mining," is nostalgia for the reliable, contractually predictable exchange that took place with a recognizable set of actors. The new private companies that have come in their place are unintelligible to the locals (who complain that it is impossible to find out who really owns them and speculatively identify them as being from "the abroad"). The commercial activities of these companies restructure and exploit nature through practices most often captured with a single condemning word, the one uttered by Oleg—bezpredel—which echoes the affective symbolism of za granitsu. Both za granitsu and bezpredel symbolize the new, expanded, unknown and unknowable modalities and networks of exchange of natural resources that have supplanted the established and recognizable commodity chains.

To wrap up this chapter, let us return to the Vepsian cosmology of Masters—as explained in Chapter 2, the nature and the function of these of forests and lakes was always regulatory. They regulated their domains of nature, as well as human behaviour, especially pertaining to different forms of exchange: offerings, contracts, appropriate forms of give-and-take between people and nature, between people and other people. For Veps, there has always existed a kind of slippage between their metaphysical Masters and the institutional Masters: the tsar, the Soviet state, the mining companies. The bad behaviour of the new companies, with their new economic regime, has mapped onto this cosmological slippage in a way that is historically unique, yet perfectly maintains what Evans-Pritchard called the "internal logic" of a cosmological belief. The new Masters have made the spaces of the forest uninhabitable for the old Masters. Metaphorically speaking, although Masters are imagined to be suprahuman, ultimately, this way of speaking about the regime change is a commentary on what Veps perceive to be an inhumane way of managing human-nature relations and resource extraction—one that is predicated on concentrated profit that bypasses them and that has no use for the cultivation and maintenance of multigenerational social ties.

Notes

1. From 1914 to 1924, the name of St. Petersburg.
2. In subsequent interviews I pursued this line of inquiry from the get-go.
3. In Russian *arendatori-megapol'zovateli* (literally, renters–mega-users).
4. The issues of nostalgia and idealization brought up by such narratives are discussed later on.
5. Veps stoneworkers, famous for their skill with raspberry quartzite, regularly accompanied the mineral to elite construction sites.

CHAPTER 5

THE LONG NIGHT
OF MUSEUMS

The Long Night of Museums has come to Sheltozero. The Long Night of Museums (also known as European Night of Museums), sponsored by the International Council of Museums (ICOM) throughout Europe and held every year on the Saturday closest to International Museum Day (celebrated worldwide on May 18), has become increasingly popular in Russian metropolitan centres like Moscow and St. Petersburg. It has also caught the attention of Nataliya, Lyudmila, and Valentina—the director and workers of the Sheltozero Vepsian Ethnographic Museum—who have devised a way to adapt this fairly new, trendy, largely urban event to a small, rural museum. And so, in late May, as the sun sets over the hill beyond the small river that divides the village, the Vepsian ethnographic museum is, for the first time, preparing for its very own Museum Night.

From an anthropological perspective, this Museum Night turned out to be an event that lent itself well to a classical "event ethnography"—an occasion that clarified the symbolic and emotional work the museum performed for present-day Sheltozero. For me, as an ethnographer, this was a particularly interesting happening because, although while living in Sheltozero I had almost daily opportunities to see how the museum played a role in the community as both an informal meeting space and an educational centre for secondary school students, most of its formal events were oriented toward outsiders. Museum Night not only turned out to be an organized, formal affair oriented toward the local community, rather than visitors, but also rendered visible the subtle work of making local life experiences into curated memories and public culture.

I had first heard about Museum Night plans at a workshop I attended with museum is director, Nataliya Ankhimova, at the National Museum of the Republic of Karelia, in Petrozavodsk. The workshop was a best practices exchange from various museum workers and other cultural sector employees in the republic, with presentations that highlighted recent projects and accomplishments of the small museums scattered throughout Karelia. Because I had helped Nataliya prepare the PowerPoint slides for her presentation, and because by that point in my stay in Sheltozero I was regularly documenting museum events for both my own ethnographic purposes and the museum's own archive of its work, I came into Petrozavodsk from the village with Nataliya to film her presentation.

Nataliya's presentation was a review of the museum's major projects of the past 15 years, beginning at the point when the museum's focus shifted from fulfilling a more antiquarian mission to being a platform for special projects, collaborative research projects, and network-building. I listened to her overview with interest; some of the projects she was detailing were already familiar to me, while others were new. I give a brief overview of them below to offer a better understanding of the museum's history and its role in producing and representing Vepsian culture in general and the culture of Sheltozero in particular, and to better situate the idea of Museum Night within the repertoire of museum's work.

Nataliya started out by revisiting the museum's first major project of the post-Soviet era—the moment in time that brought various reconfigurations in funding but also allowed for new opportunities and experimentation with the museum format. This project culminated in 1999 and was called Vepsian Land. The goal of the project was to make a "journey" through Vepsian land interesting for schoolchildren inside and outside the museum. As Nataliya explained, "That was the first time we could do walking and bus tours through Vepsian villages in Karelia and in the adjoining Leningradskaya Oblast'." As mentioned in Chapter 1, the Veps comprise three ethnic subgroups: Northern Veps (the subject of this book, also known as Onega Veps), Middle Veps, and Southern Veps.

Although they share the same language (with some dialect variations) and the same symbolic culture, Northern Vepsian communities were significantly different from the other Vepsian settlements, through different histories of subsistence and their social effects. Northern Veps were the only ones to mine and work with stone; they also practiced othodnichestvo[1] much more than their more southern brethren—as a result, their sense of self has historically been as a relatively mobile rather than rooted people. Beyond that, Russian scholars have noted that gender roles played out differently among the Northern Veps, with women being far more active in the political life of the villages than in the other Vepsian enclaves—presumably because much of village governance and decision-making fell to women while the men were absent for prolonged periods of time, working at jobs that took them away from their villages and farms. While the men were away, the women

essentially kept the villages running, both practically and administratively. As
A. Bolshakova (2012: 132–33) writes,

"In the areas where men … were absent on labour migration tasks, from early spring
until late autumn, the entire burden of agricultural labour, including plowing, sowing,
reaping, mowing, preparing stacks of hay, repairing fences, all fell on the shoul-
ders of women, teenagers, and children. A vivid description of the impact of that is
found in the Olonets government digest from 30 July 1909: 'On the West bank of
Lake Onega, there are villages where from early spring till late autumn, almost all
men are absent, they leave for jobs as stoneworkers, and a strange picture presents
itself—all field and house jobs are performed by women … a woman walks behind
a plow, a woman sows, a woman erects fences.'"

Such differences are in one way or another documented in local museums
and oral histories, allowing visitors to different Vepsian communities a comparative perspective and, especially, illuminating for Sheltozero Veps the more
subtle impacts their involvement with the mining industry has had on their
cultural history.

This project had a visual component, and the village's kids were enrolled
as participants in not only the project but also the ethnographic documen-
taries it generated. "We got the first audio and video technology," Nataliya
recalled, showing stills of these films to the audience at the workshop, "so
the same kids who would go on tours would later see themselves on a TV
screen—it was exciting for them. And the films *Ryurik*[2] *and his Sheltozero* and
Ryurik and his Museum were created thanks to this project." Although the
parameters of the project were local—Vepsian schoolchildren visiting Vepsian
villages—the project was designed with an eye for establishing and strengthening external connections and networks, especially with the Moscow cultural
sector. Transcending the regional level, the Journey project (or Vepsian Land
project), thanks primarily to its cinematic output, circulated all the way to
Moscow, resulting in Lonin receiving 3,000 rubles in funding for the museum
in 2000—a not insignificant grant amount for a tiny provincial museum, and
a symbolically important one as well for the morale of the museum workers.

The exhibit that followed, partially thanks to the secured funding, was
called *Ozhivshiy Musey* (A Museum Come to Life). That exhibit marked the
moment, explained Nataliya, when "we understood that the museum collection
has to include contemporary objects, and today, in our exhibit, we have tools
of the workers of today, alongside old artifacts—so that they can recognize
themselves in the museum, not just their grandfathers and great-grandfathers."
Nataliya credits the Vepsian Choir with aiding and, in a way, paralleling the
process of updating both the museum rooms and the mentality that a museum

is a place of salvaged culture, left behind in the past: "Our partner, a creative collective, the Vepsian National Choir, 70 years old this year—they have been singing in the museum a long time, for schoolchildren, students, adults, foreign tourists." The Vepsian Choir, a living, breathing, singing repository of cultural forms designated as "traditional" has been "modernizing" continuously, adding creative innovations and modern twists to old-time arrangements over the years. Vepsian songs have not remained static, and, over time, the museum has taken the same kind of dynamic perspective on previously circumscribed categories such as "subsistence tools" and "crafts."

The museum's portfolio includes some less "classic," even intentionally designed and curated projects; nevertheless, museum workers recollect them with pride. I had already heard about "the Vepsian wedding" from every single museum worker during my stay in Sheltozero—and saw the festive photo albums more than once—but I was still initially a bit surprised to see that Nataliya had included it into her overview of museum achievements. However, in retrospect, my surprise was misplaced; all forms of translocal connections and events were markers of prestige for the museum and the village community, who, like many of the post-Soviet indigenous groups, have on the one hand adopted the discourse that historically considered them rural and "backwards" but on the other hand were also participating in the symbolic and material practices that have, in the post-Soviet era, been articulated as cultural survival or cultural revival. With the livelihoods of both museums and the villages that contain them so tied to politically and economically significant connections across space—in the case of Sheltozero, connections with Moscow, St. Petersburg, and Finland—any kind of connection with or recognition coming from those places is simultaneously a confirmation that they are not merely provincial and backward, and evidence of and contribution toward cultural revival. So, at the museum conference, Nataliya was pleased to recall how in 2006, a couple from Moscow decided to hold a traditional Vepsian wedding for their own nuptials, mobilizing the museum, and indeed the whole village for this affair, attended by all of their friends and relatives from the capital:

> How it happened was: the groom and the bride, Kirill and Alexandra, they came to Karelia for several years in a row, travelled through our villages, in our houses, they made friends, and as you can see Moscow decided to celebrate the most important day in life in Karelia, not in any restaurant, but in our usual Karelian village ... everything was very beautiful and with specific rituals which used to happen at Vepsian weddings. You can see how one of the "wise women"—in this case the leader of the Vepsian Choir—is preparing the bride for the moment when the groom will first see her in wedding attire. Everything was done according to old traditions,

the father and the mother, the friends of the groom, all of them came and played out their roles in the museum. Under the white tablecloth—it was a good celebration, with song, dance, and a real Vepsian table.

For Nataliya and the rest of the museum workers, the bride and the groom are Moscow personified, and the unambivalent delight and pride that the Vepsian wedding—still talked about in the village—generated also reveals something important about small-numbered indigenous communities' understanding of their position in the larger Russian socio-geographical landscape. Concerns about cultural appropriation or cultural commodification are, in general, not part of indigenous cultural politics in this region of Russia (and arguably throughout Russia). And although, of course, like all brokers of indigenous culture worldwide, the museum is concerned with how its people are represented, the concern of the Sheltozero museum is more about visibility as a threshold platform to aspire to before, or at least simultaneously with, the issues of particular kinds of representation. With the understanding that as all cultural spaces, Vepsian villages like Sheltozero are sites of curated self-representation (with women doing the bulk of cultural and representational labour to the outsiders), it is a real and shared narrative within Sheltozero that Veps want to be visible and known. Even the miners I spoke to, the men of the village, although generally distanced from the cultural labour of representation, had an occupational ancestral referent of being known—even renowned— for the minerals of the region and the skills associated with them. For this generation of miners, that kind of renown is part of their professional legacy, their patrimony, in a sense. As discussed in Chapter 4, the very real crisis that Vepsian villages are experiencing around the privatization of the mining and logging industries in the region stems from their erasure from the commodity webs running through the region. The economic fallout from that is important but so is the cultural "refusal of relation" on the part of the mining companies, as a result of which Veps—historically rescued from the general backwardness ascribed to rural indigenous populations through their production of and skill with the most public and cosmopolitan mineral in the land—have lost their prestige and status. Another facet of the same dynamic is visible in the work of the museum. Villagers are proud to be associated, through the stone from their territories, with the Moscow metro, famous cathedrals, and war memorials. They are also proud to be linked, through hosting a wedding or through an ongoing research relationship, to Moscow or Finland—or France. As was previously mentioned, one of the highlights of the museum is the photographic diptych by French photographer Georges Azra: the images of Napoleon's sarcophagus, made out of raspberry quartzite, and the image of

Vepsian landscape, made by the same photographer during his visit to Karelia, side by side. The two pieces are equally significant: a piece of a Vepsian prestige object is forever linked to the French nation, while conversely, a piece of French culture is embedded in the museum, through the gift of the photo depicting a familiar vista seen through French eyes.[3] Similarly, Nataliya is just as proud of "Moscow" coming to celebrate a wedding in Sheltozero as she is of the 2009 exhibit which took "almost 200 objects" from the museum to the local capital, Petrozavodsk, where they were exhibited for two and a half months.

Nataliya's overview of the museum's history is a chronicle of such connections established and negotiated, themselves becoming a part of the village history and consequently a part of the museum archive. In many ways, the work of the museum reflects and documents Vepsian crafting of identity and place in the later Soviet and post-Soviet years. And the latest special event the museum is organizing—that Nataliya previews at this workshop—is Museum Night for Sheltozero, an event that does not aim to bring new visitors to the museum with the help of unconventional hours, but one that builds on the intimate familiarity that already exists between the village and the museum.

MUSEUM NIGHT FOR CHILDREN

Museum Night happens to fall on the night of a full moon. Yellow and plump, it hangs low in the kind of deep blue sky that is possible only far from city lights. Through the evening air, a parade of pink and blue coats and woolen hats arrives at the museum: the schoolchildren from the Sheltozero elementary and middle schools, with their teachers in tow. Museum staff—Nataliya, Lyudmila, and Valentina—have spent the entire day preparing. When I arrived at the museum a few hours earlier, video camera in hand, Nataliya was wearing the traditional Vepsian costume that she usually wears when performing with the Vepsian Choir, and the women were exchanging jokes in Vepsian—"to get into the mindset," as they explained. The Museum Night program is divided into two parts, both structured as a viktorina: a competitive game where knowledge is tested. The first part of the evening is for the children, who, upon their arrival at the museum, are split into two teams, the boys against the girls. Each team will play several rounds of the game, each tethered to a particular museum room, before they are reunited in the main communal room upstairs for kalitki[4] and tea. The assignments for boys and girls are identical, but arranged in a different order, so that they are never in the same room at the same time during the game rounds.

The girl's viktorina starts in the peasant izba. The girls, pink-cheeked from the cold, crowd around a table with their "assignment" sheets; they have to find and identify various items from a Vepsian interior, and either place them in chronological order, draw them, or correctly spell their names in Vepsian. Their first assignment is to find two kinds of irons historically used by Vepsian women—coal and brass varieties—and figure out which came first. The two irons are in clear view, positioned prominently on top of the stove, and the girls try to ascertain which one is which. One of the girls, Sasha, hems and the haws, places one hand on each, as if touching them will reveal their nature. "I think the one on the left is the coal one," ventures Alena, the tallest girl in the group. The girls eventually decide that the heaviest iron must be the brass one, and that it must also be the older one because "they would get lighter and lighter over time, wouldn't they?" They turn out to be wrong, but Nataliya consoles them: "This was a difficult question, but the game is not just to test your knowledge but for you to gain new knowledge as well."

The girls come back to the table, circle the correct answer on their worksheet, and look at their next task. That turns out to be locating the implements for spinning wool inside the izba. Curly-haired Nastya heads straight for the back room, where handspinning implements stand below antique black-and-white photographs of the once-upon-a-time residents of the izba: a husband and wife whose great-granddaughter will walk through its door later in the evening, during the grown-up viktorina. In the meantime, the girls have to locate a spinning wheel, a tow, and a spindle. As they rummage around the room, their reflections pass back and forth in the antique mirror, dim with age, flickering movement next to the stationary men and women in the sepia-toned portraits hanging around it.

They are puzzled by an oblong object with holes drilled into it. "What is it?" Nataliya prompts them. The girls demur, unsure. Finally, Nastya whispers,

Figure 5.1 Peasant *izba*

"*Shtuchka.*"[5] "*Shtuchka?*" Nataliya raises her eyebrows in mock shock. "Is that what it is called? Think about it—have you seen these at your grand-mothers' houses?" she presses, and the girls fall silent, mentally scanning the interiors of their grandmother's homes, not that different from the izba they are in. While several of the girls' grandparents have moved into the "modern" apartments behind the main village store, with central heating and indoor plumbing, most of their grandparents' homes are traditional log houses, filled with things that, once in the museum, become artifacts. A previously silent girl, Afimia, remembers knitting implements that her grandmother has handy: a hook, different sizes of knitting needles, and a special device for organizing and holding them. The girls nod, and use that information to figure out the purpose of the *shtuchka*; it is a device to hold felting needles and yarn of different sizes. Again, they circle back to the table and diligently draw the object, checking with each other how to spell "spindle" (*värtin*) in Vepsian. Eventually, at Nataliya's suggestion, everyone heads upstairs to check on the progress of the boys' team.

The boys are finishing a game in a very different medium—they are playing a multiple-choice game on the museum computer, where they have to identify Vepsian vocabulary words, find answers to Vepsian riddles, and move around squares to assemble them into familiar and significant land-scapes. As we walk into the room, after some manipulation with the mouse, a photograph of purple-pink appears, filling the monitor: raspberry quartzite, familiar to everyone in the village from childhood. "Now, where is it mined?" asks Lyudmila, who is shepherding the boys' team through their round of questions. "In Shoksha"[6] all the kids answer in unison. In the difference between the assignments designed for the girls and the boy we can see an implicit celebration and reproduction of gendered work; it is notable that the girls in the game are quizzed on objects and practices of domestic life, while the boys have to answer questions about mining.

Next, Ilya, who is sitting down at the computer, tries to get the trees and the skies to align in a picture of a baroque-looking tree known as "the tree of happiness" on the shore of Lake Onega, on the northeastern outskirts of the village. "I climbed that tree," whispers someone behind me. The squares are properly positioned, and the computer generates a "Hooray, that is correct!" message, complete with a smiley face.

The game on the screen then changes to riddles. Throughout my stay in Sheltozero, I heard many times that Vepsian riddles are unique in how esoteric and inaccessible they are—a point of tacit pride. Indeed, while generally decent at riddles, I could not crack the code of Vepsian riddles; they appeared to me self-contained and impenetrable, although highly poetic. "Ivan is crying on a mountaintop" would turn out to be a burning candle. "Two kinds of wine in a barrel" would be revealed to be an egg. "It's very simple," I would be told, "The white and the yolk are the two kinds of wine, and the eggshell is a barrel. What else could it be?" When I was frustrated at not being able to solve riddles, my friends in Sheltozero would console me by saying that one needed a *Vepsskiy sklad uma*—in literal translation, a Vepsian design of mind, or what in English would be called a mentality—to be able to understand what the images stood for. The boys breeze through a series of puzzles, with the help of multiple-choice images. Marina reads, in Russian and then, below it, in Vepsian, "It bows, it bows, it will come to the corner and stretch out," with three images pictured below: a rake, a saw, and an axe. The children brainstorm, until they correctly identify the axe as the "bowing" item. The next puzzle, "fire burning in a lake," turns out to be a samovar (a traditional Russian metal urn with a spigot used for boiling water and making tea). "Marya and Darya[7] look at each other" is the ceiling and the floor. The boys make sure to read every puzzle in Vepsian before answering; their teacher, Anna Anatolyevna, watches with a smile, and helps them out when they stumble. All the boys are diligently pronouncing Vepsian syllables, even though for some of them it is not the language spoken at home. While the girls are all from Vepsian families, the boys' group includes a Ukrainian-Armenian boy, named Armyan, who is actually wearing a shirt that says "Armenia."

These kids represent the growing diaspora of labour migrants to this region; there is some tension between them and the village old-timers. Ukrainian

Figure 5.2 Armyan acting out the "Marya and Darya" riddle

workers tend to be involved in new logging operations that Sheltozerians are vocally unhappy about, while Armenian migrants have taken over the stone-processing facilities by the lakeshore—a business that was traditionally part of the Vepsian labour flow involving regional stone production. However, as the labour flow became disrupted after privatization, various new actors appeared on the scene, from Kazakh and German quarry owners to Armenian stone processors. But while tensions may exist, the kids of these migrants attend the village school, and learn how to speak Vepsian, how to solve Vepsian riddles.

"The mother is fat, the daughter is red, the son is curly-haired." The boys pantomime the final puzzle and conclude that it is a stove (metaphorically giving birth to fire and smoke). As the game comes to an end, with the children eventually solving all the riddles, Nataliya puts on a recording of the Vepsian National Choir and says, "The Vepsian National Choir is singing especially for you—because you did such a good job."

After a few more rounds, the viktorina draws to a close, with a final assignment involving "deciphering a message from Vepsian ancestors"—a translation assignment that results in a letter to the children asking them to respect their elders and the spirit Masters, and to treasure their land and nature. Then the children are gathered before a wall of photos, with quotes by Sheltozerians and other Veps from the region, from kindergartners to the activists described in Chapter 4, commenting on their Vepsian identity.

Nataliya encourages the children to pay special attention to the photos and captions of kids, who "were still in kindergarten when we did this project, but now they are your classmates!" "Look at Liza," she continues. "What does she say?" pointing at the photo of a small girl in a black woolen cap. "I like to talk about animals in Vepsian," one of the boys, Artem, reads out loud. "And what does Katya Gerchina say?" asks Anna, the teacher. "Go ahead, read it," she says to another boy, and he leans down to read the caption under the photo of a girl who looks to be five or six. "I like to look at pictures of animals and birds. It's beautiful here [in the museum], there are toys, and tools." Another boy, Leva, is called to task. "What does Dasha, from the first grade, say?" He peers at the collage: "She says something in Vepsian." He slowly reads, one syllable at a time, and then translates: "A bat flies at night and sleeps during the day."

Nataliya directs the children to look at the photos of some of the adults in their lives—including Olga Kokorina, also a schoolteacher and a soprano in the Vepsian Choir, and the wife of the miner who first explained the concept of the "bad masters" to me. A girl reads out loud: "Olga Kokorina, she says, all my ancestors were Veps, I cannot imagine myself being a different nationality. I know the language, the culture, the traditions—I respect my people.

Figure 5.3 Reading quotes from the collage

We were all accustomed to each other, we worked together in the fields, the houses, we lived in harmony, we respected our elders." Then, finally, a caption by a young boy gets read out loud. He says "I like playing Vepsian games and hearing stories about *izand* (Khozyain)."

The kids spend a little more time in front of the collage, identifying the faces and locating them within the village kinship network. "That is Vladik.... Is he Veta's cousin? No, he is her brother." "That is our mathematics teacher.... She is your aunt, right?" Not everyone is a relative, but everyone is known. "Do you recognize him?" asks Ksenia, pointing at the photo of an unsmiling old man with severe features. "That is Uncle Vasya, who lives by the store. Did you know he participated in World War II? There aren't many of [veterans] left—have you seen him? Do you remember when we went to the Palace of Creativity and you saw his photo there? He was wearing lots of medals. And he is a Veps. He was born here, grew up here, speaks Vepsian."

The mention of World War II is not trivial. Part of the history of Sheltozero is its time under the Finnish occupation during World War II, and in school the kids are already learning the complicated wartime narrative of Finnish soldiers considering the Veps to be "their own," treating them better than their Russian captives, and even offering to take them along as they eventually retreated. The village narrative around that is one of Vepsian loyalty to their land and to the Soviet state, but also gratitude that the passage of decades has allowed them to have close relationships with Finnish "partners" these days. Meeting Finnish researchers visiting the museum as a part of cultural exchange projects today and learning what it meant to be a Veps, with tested loyalties during World War II, are both parts of local identity. The museum integrates them into a balance between historical memory and contemporary practice, and from an early age, kids learn to do so as well.

Under the photo of Valentina, herself one of the museum workers, she explains that her father was a Veps, and the photo of her father is right there on the wall as well. "I grew up in a Vepsian izba, and absorbed the culture of my people from my childhood," she has been recorded as saying. Eventually they reach the photo of Ryurik Lonin, the founder of the museum, as Nataliya reverently reminds the kids. His caption reads, "All my ancestors were Veps, they knew Vepsian better than Russian. Vepsian is my native tongue."[8]

MUSEUM NIGHT FOR ADULTS

By 9 p.m. all the children have left, and, after some downtime, the adults—all women—have arrived and are ushered into the communal room. Before they congregated, looking at all the nametags, I had asked Nataliya if it was intentional that all the participants were women. She said, "Don't you see? That's how it is in our village. Men work and fish, and women take care of the cultural tasks." Indeed, in Sheltozero the informal division of labour places women as cultural workers of all stripes, with the single exception being the Vepsian Choir, which includes male singers and dancers, and a male choirmaster.

But much of "cultural work" in the village overlaps with the hospitality sector—hosting and feeding researchers who regularly come from Petrozavodsk, from Moscow, from Finland. The emotional labour involved in providing oral histories or interviews about Vepsian lore is primarily performed by women, in part because of their physical availability; their work is primarily in the house and the garden. The men, by contrast, are harder to find for interviews; they are frequently away on multi-day fishing expeditions, working in the fields, or doing 12-hour shifts for mining or logging companies operating in the area. But beyond the circumstantial consequences of gendered labour making women easily available to visiting university professors and Finnish NGO workers, cultural work is considered to first and foremost belong to the realm of education, and the educational sphere of Vepsian culture is heavily feminized. Although the most important Vepsian cultural worker and writer is undoubtedly considered to be the founder of the museum, Ryurik Lonin, the majority of Vepsian intellectuals and educators are female—from the elementary and high school Vepsian language teachers; to the women who have gone to study Vepsian language at Petrozavodsk State University, and, in time, have themselves become professors there and researchers of Vepsian culture; to the staff of the ethnographic museum, which is exclusively female. And so it is no surprise that it is all women who are now sitting on the common-room benches, awaiting Nataliya's instructions. Among them are Irina Nikolaevna Korsak (Ira),[9] whose family has a small sales business incorporated in the village; Ekaterina Mikaylovna Zyl' (Katya), an elementary schoolteacher in the Sheltozero school with a passion for local history and place names, and a former deputy of the Vepsian Volost'; Olga Vasilyevna Kokorina (Olga), her fellow schoolteacher and one of the faces in the photo collage the children were studying a few hours earlier; Nataliya Andreevna Mikulich (Nataliya M.), a member of the Vepsian Choir; and Evgeniya Nikolaevna Smirnova (Zhenya), a deputy in the village government and a former member of the Vepsian Choir.

"This is our very first Museum Night," Nataliya explains. "In Europe it has been happening for seven years, in Russia for four or five. But it's the first one for the Vepsian museum. This is the second part of the program. First the children came: first fifth-graders then second-graders. We have been playing since 6 p.m., and we want to continue that with you all. It is an evocative idea—a night of museums. It does not mean we are here all night, it means we are open at an unusual time; the idea is to get people to come here who would not normally. I know that on [May] 14, our Karelian museums competed with each other—some had 500 visitors, some 700, some up to 1,000. But our goal is different ... we are a small museum, we are not brand new to anyone in the village, but maybe we can get you to look at things a little differently, to take a journey through our own past."

The peasant izba is open once again, and all the women take seats around it. "This is how the Veps lived about 100 years ago," says Nataliya. "You have seen all these objects—more than once. But there are many objects in the museum that you have not seen ... or maybe you have seen them, at your parents' house, but you did not really register their meaning." The women, like the children before them, will have to find answers to a variety of questions and will be awarded gold stars for each correct answer. "Because it is Museum Night, we are awarding stars," quips Lyudmila.

Nataliya gathers everyone around the stove and says, "We are not just in a peasant izba, we are in a Vepsian izba—there are some important elements here that let us know we are in a Vepsian house. What are they? Please name them; you have one minute." The women start going through the options: the Red Corner, the Vepsian cradle—"*Rodnye moi,*" (my kin), Nataliya says, "Remember, it is something unique about a Vepsian house, not just any peasant house." "A distaff?" speculates Ira. "Russians have the distaff, too," Zhenya corrects her. "And the Karels," adds Nataliya M. In a few minutes, Nataliya reveals that they are looking for five objects or elements of izba design and reminds them that every object has its place: "These are things that can be present in other ethnicities' huts, but they have some crucial difference, which may lie in where they are located." The women confer and decide upon the following answers: the red curtains; the table, which must stand between two windows; long benches; the Red Corner; and the indoor chicken coop. Nataliya accepts the curtains and the table position as correct answers but notes that every other peasant hut has long benches and does not count it, as it is not an izba feature unique to Veps. She similarly rejects the Red Corner, pointing out that it is something found in the houses of all Christians in Eastern Europe, as a place for icons and candles, and thus does not fall within the scope of the question. The indoor chicken coop is also disqualified, because Russians and Karels also made use of such a design. Missed answers turn out to be a two-sided wardrobe, which divides the Vepsian izba into two on one side, and the stove, which also serves as a divider on the other side, separating the "clean" part of the izba from the kitchen. The last object is the Vepsian floor rug, unique in the way it is striped and the colors used. I note with interest that the opening round of the game pivots on differentiation between Veps and other ethnicities, highlighting a historically important aspect of cultural articulation. During the years when indigenous languages were largely suppressed and various forms of village life were standardized through a Soviet collective farm model, these small material practices became sites of cultural differentiation and cultural uniqueness, especially for several Baltic-Finnish peoples among the Finno-Ugric ethnolinguistic group (Karels, Veps, Izhors, et cetera), who, in Soviet discourse and textbooks, were grouped together under the undifferentiated umbrella term chud' (strange ones, other ones).

The next round of the viktorina asks the women identify correct placements for various members of the Vepsian family around the table. "You have dishes prepared by our local artisans. Out of these, pick—pick what would have to be on every table, in its proper place." The women pick up and carry the objects, discussing where they would be in their proper place. "Ladies," asks Valentina, "Where would the mistress of the house sit?" The master of the hut would sit at the head of the table, and the mistress always to his right. This helps the women place the samovar on the table, and rotate it so that its nose is facing toward the seat of the woman in the house, who would pour tea for everyone.

Instead of giving the correct answers once the minute is up, Nataliya says, "You will see how well you did once you complete the next assignment" and hands out pieces of paper to each player that assign them a specific family role in the kinship matrix of a Vepsian family. A heated debate ensues over where the mistress of the house must sit if she has to be positioned to the right of her husband but also has to be able to easily get up and serve everyone throughout the meal.

Where must the daughter-in-law, the wife of the oldest son, sit if she has to help her mother-in-law? The placement is agreed upon, but then a question arises: What if she has already borne a child? The oldest male grandchild has his own place at the table, and his mother's place is relational vis-à-vis both him and her mother-in-law. The women draw on their family practices—in some cases long forgotten. As Katia whispers to Zhenya—once they are all seated properly at the table, with their designations of husband, wife, mother-in-law, younger daughter, oldest son positioned in front of them like nametags in a traditional Vepsian aged and gendered arrangement—"I haven't sat at a table like this since my grandparents died."

Next, the women are led to the computer, just like the kids were—but their task is different. They are shown photographs from the Vepsian realm, and they have to name the location of each photo. Many of the images feature churches, some active, some long out of use, like the Nativity Church in the village of Gimreka. The women don't yet know this, but this portion of the game foreshadows the excursion they will take tomorrow, which will include visits to old Vepsian churches. "Would you want to go there?" asks Nataliya, who has already planned the trip. "Well, of course," says one of the women. "*Takoye svyatoe mesto* [such a sacred place]—but it's closed." The slide-show test closes with the image of a raspberry quartzite quarry; anyone from the region would easily identify it, but especially these women, who come from

Figure 5.4 "Daughter-in-law—the wife of the eldest son"

long lines of Vepsian miners and in some cases are married into such lineages. The next assignment is aural; "You will hear three tunes," explains Lyudmila. "You will have to name the collective that sings them, the soloist, and, if you can, the name of the song." The first track is identified by Valentina as "Vova Solovyov singing that wedding song." No one is sure about the name of the collective, but everyone remembers hearing the song at Vepsian weddings, including the famous Vepsian wedding of the couple from Moscow. Later, in an interview, one of the women tells me that this song was played at her own wedding, and she is pleased that it has a place in the museum audio collection. At the opening bars of the next melody, a throaty vocalization, Zhenya sits up. "Is that my *mamanya*?" Then she shakes her head. "No, not her." The women conclude that the song is "Ruson'ka," sung by the Petrozavodsk Vepsian Choir. They are two for three, and they get two stars, When the next melody starts, everyone immediately turns and points to Zhenya, who shushes them and says, "Quiet, quiet." Everyone knows that the soloist is Zhenya's mother, a famous Vepsian singer, so rather than trying to brainstorm for the correct answer, Katia says, "Let's just sit and listen." And so they do. It is a song typical of the Vepsian choral tradition, where diaphonic and polyphonic chanting alternate, with the use of close intervals, creating a wistful, dissonant sound. Zhenya nods her head and tears up. By the time the track ends, all the women are singing along.

Next comes an "individual round"—women can earn stars on their own. Each gets a question, and they have to locate the answer somewhere in the exhibition hall. The questions range from "Locate the books of R.P. Lonin" to "Find the strange creature borne by the forest, and name its Master." As some women are still looking for their answers, Zhenya and Katia have stopped in front of the board that houses the photographs of the different incarnations of the Vepsian National Choir and the Vepsian Children's Choir. "Look at them. They are so little, so sweet," says Katia of a relatively recent photo, which features her own kids; immediately above it is an older sepia photo— the version of the choir in which Zhenya' s mother was a soloist, the continuity between what are literally voices of each generation commemorated on the museum wall. I join them and ask Zhenya about her mother—this interview, one of the several I have done with her, is spontaneous and circumstantial. "She was in the choir, and my father was, too. She really had an inimitable voice," Zhenya recalls. "And her father—adds Katia—he was an artist, too, and he received the title … either the National Worker of Culture of Karelia or Distinguished Worker of Culture of Karelia." "Distinguished, it was distinguished," Zhenya confirms. She continues, "At home we keep an autograph from the original founder of the Vepsian Choir—there he is, right there"—she points to a man on the right side of the sepia photo—we have an autograph, written in his own hand—"to the best *zapevala* [soloist] of the Vepsian National Choir. Inimitable voice she had, there is no other like it. And," she continues, "the museum of course has all the recordings of her singing, and we have it at home, too, of course—how could we not? Both my mother and my father were in the choir, and I see myself in these pictures, on these walls, too." She points to a younger version of herself in the photo from 1992 and identifies her sister in the same group as well. "I am about 30 in that photo. And up here"—she points to the older photo of her mother— "that's me, too, about five months in utero." She goes back to the later photo, looking for her mother, but does not see her. "She must have walked away right then," she muses. "My son was very little then, and he would have been in the photo, too, but he was probably running off, and she went with him. My sister's little daughter was also there. She must have gone with the both of them." To Zhenya, the photograph is not just a museum commemoration of the different epochs of the "national treasure," as the choir is often called. The photo brings memories of the time when her son was small, her mother was alive—it is a family photo for her, and for many of the villagers who find themselves in the museum, whether for museum activities (infrequently) or community and social events (quite often). The photos do not attract attention, but people can pause in front of them, find their parents and grandparents, and feel the fluid interplay between intimate family and village culture and official "museum culture." The fluidity between these two domains simultaneously enables the functioning of the "living museum" as it reflects back the intimate, the familiar, the relevant and immediate aspects of its visitors' lives—and it helps Vepsian children learn from an early age that the Vepsian nation is such a small community that their families' lives, as such, count as both "politics" and "culture," and are commemorated accordingly. For someone like Zhenya, the link is even more literal and immediate. As she says, "I come here often, because the museum—the building itself—it was the house of my great-great-grandfather. He was the one who built it. So when I am here—it is like I am in my own house. That other half [of the gallery room], where we were earlier—my grandmother lived there, even during my lifetime. I visited her here, when I was six, seven, eight. She lived there, and she died there, too."

While the women wander around the gallery, reminiscing over photos and paging through books and dictionaries, Nataliya and Lyudmila tally the score so far; the women have gathered 37 stars out of a possible 42. Now the time has come for the final part of the game, which takes place in the exhibition room where subsistence tools are featured. The women are given different objects and cooperate to identify the links between them; it turns out that they are all traditional Vepsian musical instruments used by Ryurik Lonin, including flat, black stones from the shores of Lake Onega. Then the game is over, and the women head back into the community room for tea. As we walk in, Zhenya points to the pencil-and-charcoal framed drawing of a redhead and says to me, "That is my mother; this is a portrait of my mother, Muza Timofeevna. She does not look exactly like herself, but I guess that is how she posed. The pose, how she is sitting—it's all her, how the body is positioned. The face is not an exact likeness." Zhenya explains that her mother had posed for a student from the St. Petersburg Academy of the Arts:

> The students came here, drew everything here—nature—everything—then they visited our house with their teacher, Academic Vitergonsky. He stayed with us often; he liked my parents, and we had a fantastic banya, so he kept coming back, especially in the winter—he steamed himself and rolled around in the snow. The girls, his students came, one of them liked my mother and decided to draw her portrait. Mama posed for her, and maybe she was a little bit shy or embarrassed; that is why the face came out wrong. When you come by my house, I will show you some better portraits of her—or maybe the museum has some. Her face, in real life, was softer than [this portrait]—she was very beautiful.

I ask her: How did the portrait end up in the museum? She recalls that the original drawing was a sketch, done for their teacher:

> And when the students left, this particular girl worked on the portrait some more, and when the exhibition from the academia came here, among the works was my mother's portrait. I asked to be gifted this portrait, for my house, but then this entire series of drawings actually ended up being gifted to the museum. So these works, including the portrait of my mother, will now be exhibited in our museum, so we can go and gaze on our own, like me with my mother.... Of course, I would have bought it for my house, but that's okay.... I told you, the museum is almost like my house anyway; when I come here, I feel like I am returning to my childhood, because it is my ancestors' house. And I have objects from the museum, well, the house, in my home, too: I have an icon that was a memento, from when my grandmother lived there; the others are still in the museum, but one is in my house, the icon of my grandmother. She brought it from [St.] Petersburg, of Saint Cosmas and Damian, from the eighteenth century.

After the game ends, the women sit down for tea at a table properly positioned between two windows, teasing each other about their "family positions" based on how they sit around the table, apropos of the earlier game:

Figure 5.5 Zhenya with the portrait of her mother

"Oh, you must be my daughter-in-law! Quick, serve me!" Tea is being poured, and Nataliya emerges from her office with a stack of papers. "A very important moment has come: very soon, in an hour and a half, it will be May 18, Museum Day, and today you brought us tremendous enjoyment with your knowledge, your interest in today's event—and I think what you see in this book will delight you." "You already have," yell out the women. Nataliya continues: "The Museum Collective is awarding you a ticket for a journey— a journey through the lands of the ancient tribe of Veps. Let me read it out loud: 'This ticket is awarded to the victors in the educational museum viktorina for adults, the participants of the cultural program Museum Night in the Vepsian Museum, in coordination with an all-European Museum Night, which happened on May 17. The ticket is valid until June 17.' Today with great pleasure I turn over this ticket to you, and today, over this festive table, we will start discussing when we can go on this journey. The itinerary of the journey is: Sheltozero, Drugaya Reka [Other River], Kaskisruchey, Gimreka, Shcheleyki.[10] Then we will return to Sheltozero. And now time has come to open the wine and fill our glasses."

A JOURNEY THROUGH THE LAND OF THE ANCIENT TRIBE OF VEPS
Over wine and snacks at the museum, the promised journey was scheduled for the very next day. "Why wait?" was the refrain. People felt that if the trip was put off, the momentum and the energy from Museum Night would dissipate,

and everyone would get too busy with their household tasks to take a day off. And so, the following morning, the women gather in front of the house of Olga Kokorina, the schoolteacher-soprano, married to Oleg, the miner introduced in Chapter 4. It is drizzling lightly, and the school bus commandeered for this purpose arrives and promptly breaks down. The school bus driver leaves and returns with a multi-purpose van used to transport, at various times, the schoolchildren and the miners, and sometimes loaned out to the department of forestry. The mood among the women is jovial and festive, despite the fact that the day is gray and the rain is picking up. If yesterday's evening in the museum facilitated a journey in time for these Vepsian women, today the final, daytime segment of the Museum Night endeavour has made it possible for them to move through space—up to, and even slightly beyond, the historical borders of the ring of villages their parents and grandparents came from, once drawn by the industrial possibilities around Sheltozero. Ivan, a former miner turned bus driver and conscripted for the day, keeps asking Katia, "But tell me, why are you going?" "Just because," she replies, coquettishly. "No, that's not possible," he shakes his head. "People don't go on trips like these just because. It must be some special occasion."

As the school bus pulls out, Nataliya starts narrating the excursion: "We are departing on a journey to Vepsian Land. Today, on this holiday, we are going on the ancient road laid from Petrozavodsk to Vytegra in the seventeenth century. So imagine—it's been around for four centuries. Once upon a time, this road was called *Mirskaya* [Worldly], and it is because it was built by the whole world. If you remember, there were work assignments back then, like public works now, and our ancestors built this road. Maybe from the museum photos you remember that it was a hard road to pass. Here, I have some photos with me." "And it remains difficult to pass to this day," quips someone from the back of the bus. Everyone laughs. The roads are harsh here, everyone is used to bumping along on regional buses without shocks, and pushing one's own or a neighbour's car out of the mud is a regular occurrence. The road conditions have especially deteriorated in the last decade, thanks to the combination of cuts in federal funding to the region and the constant stream of large trucks carrying slabs of stone, something the villagers are very aware of, as discussed in Chapter 4. "And partially because of how impassable the roads were, the best of transports for the Veps historically was water transport—a boat." Nataliya passes around more photos from the museum archives, these ones of water transport infrastructure in the 1940s, pointing out where boats travelling between villages docked. "Incidentally," she continues, "today we will go to places where centuries-old pines grow—those places were called Shipping Places in the past because those trees were logged for the building of

Figure 5.6 Looking at archival photos on the field trip

the tsar's navy." The women nod, recalling a familiar and impressive fact: the smooth purple-pink gloss of raspberry quartzite isn't the only thing that historically linked Vepsian villages to the seats of power. As discussed in Chapter 3, Vepsian timber was the raw material for royal warships, starting in the days of Peter the Great.

As we move along, more historical landmarks come into focus and disappear: a cluster of former villages on land settled a long time ago because of its healing springs, with water containing high levels of iron—similar to the famous Martial Springs described in Chapter 3. These villages were demolished in the 1960s, during the urbanization campaign that affected many Vepsian communities in the region. But today, Nataliya explains, "In memory of the people who once lived there, these houses still stand—and some of them are even becoming inhabited again, part time." "Do we know the families who lived there?" asks Irina. "We know some, the ones that have come to the museum," replies Nataliya. As children and grandchildren of the Veps resettled from these villages have begun to return, at least during the summers, the museum is a community resource for them, to help them reconstruct village layout and holdings—in some cases for sentimental value, in other cases to help with researching and negotiating family land titles.

Continuing in her role as tour guide, Nataliya points out the window. "On our right, we are passing…" "A garbage dump," says Zhenya, finishing her sentence. Indeed, large garbage dumps can periodically be seen through the bus windows, the legacy of logging brigades and transient mining workers in the area. "We are not looking at the dump, we are looking at the beautiful things,"[11] continues Nataliya, unperturbed. "We are focusing on our ancestral forests, and on our orchards. Note the apple trees here; [the village of] Rybreka has always been famous for them. And why did they grow here? Because in the past it was like a garden here, this whole region. Apples, plums, cherries— they were fertilized and cultivated, and residents of the village could request trees for their land, and get saplings."

We spend the day slowly making our way south, hearing historical facts and lore about the old villages, some still half-inhabited, some all but disappeared. As our route takes us down the eastern shore of the lake, we stop and walk down to the water several times, weaving our way through brambles. But these are just interludes. The highlight of our trip, for the women, is the visit to an old church in the village of Gimreka, preceded by a brief visit to another church in the neighbouring settlement of Shcheleyki. The entire district is famous for its wooden ecclesiastical architecture and for the churches in these villages, dating back to the seventeenth and eighteenth centuries. The churches are not in use, although the one in Gimreka holds services on special holidays. To get into the churches, we visit with elderly locals who have the keys to the buildings—a very old woman in Gimreka, and a very old man in Shcheleyki. "As if in a fairy tale!" exclaims Katia excitedly; "I remember, I passed by this village in 1988, but did not even see the church. But I heard about it, and always wanted to see it."

The school bus cannot take us up to the churches. In Gimreka, we disembark in the middle of a path and walk toward the wooden domes across a field. "Do people still live along this road?" asks Olga. "*Dachniki,*" says Nataliya, referring to people whose primary residences are in cities but who use village houses as summer homes and maintain orchards and garden plots.

This region also suffered the demolition of the villages several decades ago, and today it is peppered with small Vepsian settlements where the population has shrunk to 60 or 70 people.

The Shcheleyki Church of Dimitri Solunski[12] was built in 1793. It consists of the main building and the bell tower, connected by a wooden bridge. The five-domed construction houses an octagonal chapel, which smells of myrrh. The women reverently cross themselves as they explore the corners of the chapel, and a few climb up all the way to the top of the bell tower. The women discuss how beautiful the church is and how dilapidated it is becoming. But there are signs of life; someone has been inside recently. There is a bouquet of pussy willows, and a painted egg left over from the recent Russian Orthodox holidays: Pussy Willow Sunday[13] and Easter.

The view from the bell tower jogs Ira's memory: her friend's grandmother once lived in this village. She points to the landscape. "We used to run around there as children—through all those fields, down to the water—wherever we wanted; we only took caution with the forest," she says, echoing the reverent respect, grounded in belief and superstition, for the forest as a place where physical and spiritual worlds overlap. These beliefs are still robust today, as shown in Chapters 2 and 5, having survived all the different phrases of "modernization" among the Veps. The forest starts close to the church, lying between the churchyard and the shore of Lake Onega, along which a rock ridge, all made of black gabbro-diabase, arches to the northeast.

We don't linger in Shcheleyki, though, because Nataliya wants to make sure we make it to the Gimreka pogost[14] before the sun starts to set. This famous pogost around the Church of the Nativity of the Sacred Mother of God, built in 1695, is visible from afar, as it was built on a hill rising up above the village.

Because of its elevation, it has historically served as an orientation landmark for local fishermen. And after another short bus ride and a long walk up a hillside, we are unlocking and entering the pogost, surrounded by a wooden fence with a gable roof and carved entrance gates. The churchyard is enclosed by a wooden fence, which has a gable roof and carved entrance gates. Much of the pogost is gone, but the church, the bell tower, and the cemetery remain. The church is typical of the region's steeled churches, with a cylindrical neck and a bulbous onion dome, covered in shingles. The key given to us by the old Gimreka woman works, and everyone takes turns walking up to the icons, crossing themselves reverently, and bowing low. I overhear prayers: For a husband, out of work. For a child's recovery from measles. For a recently diseased mother.

Then, in a whisper, Nataliya points out the architectural and decorative features of the church that show the handiwork of renowned Vepsian woodworking masters. The women touch the small holes carved in wood, and a repetitive wavy pattern that was intentional: to suggest the waves of the water, the lake, bringing traditional and subtly pagan motifs into the historical church. Nataliya then fingers the birchbark used on the windowsills of the church and comments that they catch water without rotting. "Here, too," she says, "we can be proud of the woodwork done by our masters." "Look at how beautiful it is around here," she says, leading the women out of the chapel and into the bell tower, "How far we can see, the villages, the lake."

This bell tower is more accessible than the one in the Shcheleyki church, wide open to both visitors and the elements. It is very windy, and everyone in the group is holding on to their hats and umbrellas as they survey the landscape beneath them. From here, high up on the hillside, it is as if different layers of Vepsian life experience are integrated: a landmark sacred to Veps as devout

Figure 5.7 Group photo at the Gimreka church

Orthodox Christians overlooking the forest, respected by the Veps because they also believe in forest spirits and Khozyayeva. The forest leads down to the lake that originally drew Vepsian ancestors to settle in this region, centuries ago, and parallel to it runs the black rock ridge that brings in more and more mining companies today. And all around the church is an old cemetery, some graves marked by crosses, a few—clearly dating from the Soviet era—with red stars.

There are flower offerings here and there, but most gravestones are overgrown with grass. Some are virtually invisible; the kin of the villages dispersed during the urbanization campaign. Soon, the sun will set. Soon, we will head back to Sheltozero. Nataliya M.'s phone rings; her husband is unhappy that she has been gone all day. "We are in Gimreka," she says. "Yes, Gimreka." "Are you crazy?" the phone booms. "Tell him the bus broke down," whispers someone, and Nataliya M. cracks up laughing but conceals it. "Yes, soon," she says, and hangs up. "I have to be home in an hour. He is upset because there is no dinner and I am not home."

"WE ARE LOOKING AT THE BEAUTIFUL THINGS"

Nataliya Ankhimova's constant attunement to the beauty of the Vepsian realm, and especially her casually reframing sentence when we passed the garbage dump—"We are looking at the beautiful things"—sums up much of the meaning-making work the museum does, as it has moved out of the initial "salvage ethnography" purpose with which it was founded by Ryurik

Lonin. On our way back, we stopped to take in a view of the lake at sunset, and to get to the overlook, we had to pass a pile of refuse from the quarries—a messy, mountain of stone shards and waste overwhelming the landscape. *"Chto oni tut nadelali"* [Look at the mess/disaster they made]," sighed Katia. "The forest is unrecognizable now, it's shameful," echoed Zhenya. Such observations were familiar to me. As seen in the previous chapters, discontent and anxiety about the transformation of the landscape are a consistent background to more vocal articulations of economic mistreatment the village experiences at the hands of the new quarry owners, "the bad masters." In some ways the sight was triggering to the women on a personal level, a reminder of changes that have ranged from unwelcome to devastating for many of their husbands and brothers in the mining profession.

But the discontent goes beyond that. In the last decade Veps have seen major disruptions in the visibility and mirroring of their culture and its achievements—social processes where in one way or another, for better or worse, aesthetics have been paramount. Marginalized—as most indigenous, rural peoples were during the Soviet era for beliefs and symbolic practices that the Soviet state considered to be examples of "obscurantism" and rural "backwardness"—Veps, or at least Vepsian men, heads of families, consistently saw their "value" recognized and conferred by the powers that be through material practices, the most prominent of which was stonework on a highly aestheticized mineral: those examples of "the labour of Vepsian hands" that decorated Lenin's mausoleum, Napoleon's sarcophagus, royal palaces turned into national museums, and the Moscow metro, commonly described as "the most beautiful metro in the world." With the double shift in mining practices—away from the decorative raspberry quartzite toward the functional and anonymous gabbro-diabase, and away from state-owned production, with its intergenerational job security, toward private, foreign ownership of the quarries and marginalization of Vepsian labour—Vepsian visibility and the prestige it brought was compromised. And, as mentioned at the beginning of the chapter, visibility and recognition from outside, especially "from above," was historically connected with the Vepsian sense and articulation of cultural self.

And visibility as a project has been the task of the museum for a long time, as the link between the village and those who behold and witness it. In the same way that the museum serves as a cultural broker—making Vepsian culture visible to urban museums and scholars, foreign researchers, Moscow juries, and tourists from far away with events like the Long Night of Museums—its work also makes Vepsian culture and history visible to village residents themselves. Or, rather, its work is that of converting personal life experiences and family memories into public history that gains visibility and recognition as it is exhibited and performed. As the choirmaster of the Vepsian Choir, introduced earlier, told me, "You are so ordinary, ordinary Veps, ordinary family, mama, papa, you just do your thing. And then you go to the museum, and there your family is—in the museum—that means they were something, something important. Part of history."

Notes

1. A feudal-era term meaning temporary labour migration (the word literally means "going away"); Vepsian othodnichestvo is discussed in detail in Chapter 1.

2. Ryurik Lonin, Vepsian folklorist and ethnologist, founder of the Sheltezero Vepsian Ethnographic Museum, discussed in the previous chapters.

3. In fact, this link inspired the museum to host a French-themed exhibit of Azra's work, entitled "A Walk through France." This is how the press release on the news page of the official Government of Karelia French portal described the event: "The exhibition opening in the village of Sheltozero was attended by Georges Azra and Taisia Dudinova, assistant manager. About forty local residents—schoolchildren, teachers, pensioners, housewives—gathered for the meeting. M. Azra impressed the audience with his perfect Russian language skills, lateral thinking, warm-heartedness and communication volubility. Videoclips which used Georges Azra's works followed his story about the photopictures. Because of amazing charm of the author, his unusual view of the beautiful, his love for life, participants of the meeting have made a true 'walk about France'" (http://www.gov.karelia.ru/News/2010/12/1214_09_e.html, accessed September 4, 2013).

4. Small traditional open-faced Vepsian pies, stuffed with mashed potato, millet, or barley porridge, traditionally made on Sundays or during festive occasions, but today made at the museum for tourists whenever tour groups come, and also sold commercially at the village store.

5. A word meaning, approximately, "a thingy."

6. The village down the road from Sheltozero, next to the main raspberry quartzite quarry—the stone itself is often referred to eponymously as "shoksha."

7. Common Russian and Vepsian names.

8. The paramount place of Vepsian language as a "heritage language" in Vepsian cultural survival and revival discourse is discussed in the introduction.

9. In the rest of the chapter the women are referenced by shortened first names; other women participated in the Museum Night, but only the women who are directly quoted in this chapter are identified in detail here. Nataliya Mikolich is designated as Nataliya M., to differentiate her from Nataliya Ankhimova, the director of the museum.

10. These are all nearby villages.

11. Nataliya used the turn of phrase in Russian, *my smotrim na krasivoe*, which positioned the adjective "beautiful" as a noun: "We are looking at the beautiful" would be the literal translation.

12. Russian version of Demetrius of Thessaloniki.

13. Pussy Willow Sunday is the Russian equivalent of Palm Sunday, a moveable feast that takes place the Sunday before Easter.

14. Parish centres that included a church, a cemetery, and, in the past, communities themselves. There are many abandoned pogosty in Karelia; often all that remains (as in this case) is a church and the adjoining graves.

CONCLUSION

In his famous ethnographic essay, anthropologist Clifford Geertz (1973), when describing the Balinese cockfight, explained it as a story the Balinese tell themselves about themselves. People—peoples, communities, nations—always find and invent ways to tell such stories about themselves to themselves. These stories are externalized as rituals and religious forms (as Émile Durkheim noted, religious practices essentially amounted to a society worshipping itself), as origin myths, as narratives about traumatic and formative periods in their history.

Veps are no exception: they tell stories about themselves to themselves across a variety of platforms. Even as they weave in and out of other's stories, they incorporate these mirrored reflections into their own identity. As they become a backdrop, a stage set, a theme for the wedding of sophisticated Moscow urbanites, the wedding also becomes a story of their cultural work, of the village's centrality and importance as a legible and desirable destination. Although the intersecting historical memories of World War II inscribe them in different ways in competing Soviet and Finnish stories, at that time on opposite sides of the Allies-Axis divide, Veps negotiate their own historical sense of that time period. So, cast as traitors by the Soviet powers and claimed as (more or less) lost little brethren by the Finns, Veps negotiate their own understanding of who they were during the war, and how that positionality shaped their ongoing identity politics and identity sensibilities. Despite the trauma of forced collectivization that Veps experienced, along with many other Soviet communities, many older Veps today are vested in their Soviet identity on their own terms: as a way to own their experiences, as a way to frame the genesis of their families (many, like my landlord, married labour specialists who were deployed to the village as a part of the collectivization project), and as a way to mobilize the language of the "good old times" discourse to critique the post-Soviet, privatization-related changes that are befalling their forests and their communities. As for being the ethnic kindred of Finns, Veps see affinity but also maintain distance; if anything, they use the historical works of Finnish linguists that cast Veps as Finnish "ancestors" to construe Finnish culture as derivative from their own. As one of my informants said to me, "They like to come and learn about us, Finns, but I think they are really learning from us."

A close look at Vepsian culture is a way to tell many stories. Veps are not just an instrumental mirror. Their experiences are in some ways representative of indigenous fates under Soviet and post-Soviet regimes, as they went through a long process of finding their political place in a state that had, over the long term, a mercurial and inconsistent vision of what indigeneity meant and how indigenous citizens fit into the Soviet project. Their history is also a prism through which some of the complicated ways in which World War II played out beyond the heroic narratives can be seen. The occupation of Vepsian territories by Finnish troops revealed that ethnic classification mattered in a unique way when those ethnicities could be "claimed" by enemy forces—and that very claim rendered such communities suspect both during and after the war. The heroic stories of collective farming in the region have the dark underside of having been organized through relocations of Veps (and other ethnicities)—which had a punitive aspect. Vepsian history also offers insight into how the category of ruralness intersected with the idea of indigeneity, and how cultivating an identity around a particular and unique skill (as stone-workers of a rare stone) mitigated the negative stereotypes ascribed to peasants and fleshed out communal notions of ethnic pride, seamlessly weaving a particular type of labour practices together with religious practices, linguistic practices, folklore, and material culture.

But this ethnographic case study also represents a rare example of an indigenous community that has historically claimed resource extraction as a central part of its identity. And because of that, the case of Veps must be considered as a distinctive indigenous revitalization movement. Their experiences over the past several centuries have been fundamentally different from the common narrative of indigenous experiences that is grounded in "green primitivism"— a romanticization of the connection between indigenous cultures and their natural environment, in which indigenous peoples are cast as "intuitive stewards of their natural habitat" and "natural conservationists" (Conklin and Graham 1995) organically enmeshed with their ecosystems (Barnard 1999). Such a political identity does not easily accommodate indigenous communities welcoming and engaging in extractive industries; within the parameters of green primitivism, "true" indigeneity is contingent on an opposition to extractive industries, or at least on a relationship with extractive practices that is begrudgingly accepted as a Faustian contract. These dynamics are evident in indigenous politics in Latin America among tribes like the Kayapo (Brazil) (Turner 1995) and the Cofán (Ecuador) (Cepek 2008), in Africa among the Ogoni (Nigeria) (Bob 2005), and in Asia among the Dognria Kongh (India) (Adamson 2012), to name just a few.

Partly because of historical differences in the Russian and Soviet negotiations of the nature-culture divide and human nature relations (compared to the shape those concepts took in the industrialized West) and partly because the Soviet classification system of indigeneity was based on linguistic and subsistence differences (rather than essentialist differences, which were racialized in a way that frequently cast indigenous peoples as virtually different species, more akin to local flora and fauna than to Westerners and their ideas of personhood), Veps acquired a different historical positionality with regard to "their" nature and their place in it than many indigenous communities in the post-colonial spaces of Euro-American imperialism. In a national project structured around class politics rather than ethnopolitics, indigeneity as a category of essential difference (as it figured in Euro-American spaces that did not pursue Marxist nation-building as a part of their post-colonial trajectories) was subsumed by prescriptive ideologies around class, where urban-rural and linguistic divides were far more salient than ethnic differences in terms of policy and legislation. These circumstances shaped a different intersection between extractive practices and "indigeneity" as an identity than the ones we are used to seeing in the media, through tropes of resilient but vulnerable "authentic" indigenous communities mounting resistance against interloper extractive companies. Stammler (2011) discusses this dynamic in the context of his essay on industrialization in northern Russia, where he notes that in many cases, indigenous communities in the post-Soviet milieu do not have the tradition (or the political capital) that could position them to resist extractive industries; in fact, the ideological tradition they orient themselves around is that of a Soviet collective identity that allows for, and even presupposes, the co-existence of indigenous subsistence practices and industrial development.

Thus, the Veps, who not only ideologically integrated the idea of coexistence with extractive industries in the service of the Soviet nation-building project, but, in fact, have relied on extractive industries for much of their cultural and economic capital over centuries, present a counterpart to the common image of indigenous struggles around the world—centred around David-like indigenous communities and Goliath-like extractive industries that are a recent and unwelcome force on "traditional" territories. In that, Veps challenge the pervasive and powerful, yet limiting, construct of indigeneity that comes out of the romanticism of green primitivism. Veps have for centuries relied on parallel subsistence practices of agriculture and resource extraction. As reviewed in the book, during the tsarist era, these subsistence forms were swidden agriculture and artisanal mining and logging; during the Soviet era, the Veps region was a place of kolkhozes and sovkhozes, even as people maintained their forest plots, and mining and logging were managed through state programs and actors; and in the post-Soviet years, there has been a return of small-scale subsistence agriculture and a dramatic acceleration of mining and logging, this time by private companies. At every point in this history, resources rights in the region have belonged to the different incarnations of the state, although currently the Republic of Karelia auctions off forest and mineral concessions to private companies, which then have virtually unlimited power throughout their concessions, as was shown in Chapter 4.

In *Capital*, Karl Marx (1992 [1867]) developed the concept of *Stoffwechsel*, which literally meant "exchange of substance" and has been translated into English as "metabolism." For Marx, *Stoffwechsel* literally referred to the processes of exchange of substances and materials between people and nature: the kind of metabolism that drives agricultural production, where fertilization (giving back to the soil) is necessary for harvest. As we saw in Chapter 2, Vepsian beliefs are centred on deeply entrenched regulatory frameworks of exchange, and, indeed, we can see how exchange as a protocol for understanding one's place in the world and living in a community is central to Vepsian culture. Whether in ritualized exchanges and moral contracts with the forest spirits, or in ongoing contractual exchanges between Vepsian villages and the state, this framework of exchange has historically centred around nature and its products: an egg for a safe passage for the cows and the cowherder; raspberry quartzite for status and glory; gabbro-diabase for kindergartens, health services, and other Soviet-era infrastructure. Part of the story of the recent changes that Veps have experienced has to do with that moral framework of solid exchange relationships with clear expectations and obligations being dramatically disrupted with the arrival of the new "Masters"—the private companies that operate in Vepsian territories but are legally, financially, and even physically decoupled from the region. The closed system of "exchange of matter," where the rules of exchanging nature's bounty were legible and reliable, has become disordered and ungovernable by legal or moral contracts. This particular aspect of Vepsian history offers a valuable counterpoint to the somewhat essentialized image of indigenous communities having to defend an "organic" relationship with nature against industries such as mining or logging. The Vepsian relationship with nature was centred on nature being a valuable medium of exchange. For centuries, mining for rare minerals and logging sturdy lumber of exceptional quality for the royal navy was a key aspect of the Vepsian mindful and holistic relationship with nature.

One of the questions that is implicitly asked in this book is this: When a community identity is strongly tethered to particular natural resources and an adjoining labour history, what happens when that community is disenfranchised vis-à-vis those resources? Veps are experiencing either actual dispossession or anxiety and uncertainty around their claims to both their nature and the social contract with the state that has been historically mediated through that nature. But the historical centrality of the mining and logging industries to Vepsian identity is underpinned by a vast corpus of history and memory that, in particular in Sheltozero, has found corporeal existence as material culture, with family histories centralized in the museum to coalesce into public history. This public history is a tangible mirror of the multi-faceted past for Veps, who have inhabited a shifting field of cultural identities that doubled as political categories: the state serfs in a feudal landscape, the rural proletariat, the ethnic group favoured by enemy forces during the Great Patriotic War, and the cultural workers representing and conserving their own culture in the face of aggressive urbanization and the liquidation of villages. They have also, more recently, integrated their position as a small-numbered indigenous minority transitioning from inhabiting the Soviet space of indigeneity, with its entitlements and projections, to the post-Soviet, and more international space of indigeneity, where, although many of the previous entitlements have been lost or divested, new discursive and political frameworks are available to them, including real and digital connections with indigenous activists from outside Russia, exchanging experiences and best practices for cultural survival and language revival—practices that can augment the infrastructure of cultural work and the formal labour of cultural workers that has remained robust and meaningful even in the post-Soviet period.

The museum that has been at the centre of this book is both the medium and the metaphor for the processes shaping Vepsian culture today: an integration of "folkloric" sensibilities and an antiquarian spirit in the collection of Vepsian material culture with public outreach, local curriculum building, and innovative bids for cosmopolitanism and modernity (such as Museum Night) that at the same time remain truly community-based activities—Vepsian culture for others, but first and foremost for Veps. Onega Veps can access their history in multiple ways and formats and are able to experience it as continuity, rather than rupture, between the recent and not-so-recent past, the anxious present, and the uncertain, yet in some ways hopeful, future.

GLOSSARY

Bezpredel—literally means "without boundaries" or "without a limit" and is used figuratively to criticize someone in a position of power or authority doing anything they want with full impunity

Chud'—Russian term meaning literally "different" or "others" but used in Russian folk ethno-nomenclature to refer to a group of ethnicities, including Veps

Hondole Jangele—a Vepsian term meaning "another's footprint" or "a stranger's footprint," which is used in Russian as "a bad footprint" or "the devil's footprint"—all of which pertain to becoming caught up in a punitive space-time distortion caused by Forest Masters

Khozyain / Khozyayka / Khozyayeva—literally Master/Mistress, for Veps titles for forest spirits

Kolkhoz—an abbreviation, from *kol(lektivnoe)*, or "collective" + *Hoz(jajstvo)*, or "household," a collective farm in the USSR

Korenizatsiya—literally, "putting down roots" was a policy of "indigenization" (as the Russian term for indigenous population is *korennoe naselenie*, the "rooted community") during the 1920s that was designed to establish local governance where native and indigenous leaders were promoted

Leshiy—another term for Master of the Forest (from *les*, which means "forest"), also used in Russian folklore

Othodnichestvo—literally meaning "going away," a term for feudal-era temporary labour migration

Pogost—Parish centres that included a church, a cemetery, and, in the past, communities themselves

Sovkhoz—a state-owned farm in the USSR (financed by the government, as opposed to a kolkhoz, which was self-financed)

Tsar—king

Vodyanoy—water spirit

Volost'—an autonomous municipality, etymologically derived from the old Russian word for "to possess," from which the word *vlast*, which means "power," is also derived.

Za granitsu—literally meaning "beyond the border" and used to talk about "abroad"

REFERENCES

Adamson, J. 2012. "Indigenous Literatures, Multinaturalism, and Avatar: The Emergence of Indigenous Cosmopolitics." *American Literary History* 24 (1): 143–62. https://doi.org/10.1093/alh/ajr053.

Anderson, D.G. 1991. "Turning Hunters into Herders: A Critical Examination of Soviet Development Policy among the Evenki of Southeastern Siberia." *Arctic* 3 (1): 12–22.

Anderson, D.G. 2000. *Identity and Ecology in Arctic Siberia: The Number One Reindeer Brigade*. New York: Oxford University Press.

Arnoldi, M.J. 1999. "From the Diorama to the Dialogic: A Century of Exhibiting Africa at the Smithsonian's Museum of Natural History (Du Diorama au dialogue: un siècle d'exposition sur l'Afrique au Smithsonian Museum of National History)." *Cahiers d'Etudes Africaines* 39 (155): 701–26. https://doi.org/10.3406/cea.1999.1773.

Azovskaya, L. 1977. "O Verovaniyax Vepsov." *Etnografica Narodov Vostochnoy Evropi*. L: 140–52.

Barnard, A. 1999. "Modern Hunter Gatherers and Early Symbolic Culture." In *The Evolution of Culture—An Interdisciplinary View*, edited by R. Dunnbar, C. Knight, and C. Power, 50–70. Edinburgh: Edinburgh University Press.

Bazhov, Pavel. 1948. *Malaxitovaya Shkatulka*. OGIZ.

Bird-David, N. 1999. "'Animism' Revisited: Personhood, Environment, and Relational Epistemology." *Current Anthropology* 40 (S1): S67–91. https://doi.org/10.1086/200061.

Bob, C. 2005. *The Marketing of Rebellion: Insurgents, Media, and International Activism*. New York: Cambridge University Press.

Bolshakova, A. 2012. "Traditsionnie Obyazannosti Zhenshin v Xozyaystve Vepsov vo Vtoroy Polovine XIX–nachale XX v." *Vestnik* 4 (1): 132–41.

Broz, L. 2007. "Pastoral Perspectivism: A View from Altai." *Inner Asia* 9 (2): 291–310. https://doi.org/10.1163/146481707793646566.

Burns, P. 1998. "Tourism in Russia: Background and Structure." *Tourism Management* 19 (6): 555–65. https://doi.org/10.1016/S0261-5177(98)00060-0.

Cepek, M.L. 2008. "Essential Commitments: Identity and the Politics of Cofán Conservation." *Journal of Latin American and Caribbean Anthropology* 13 (1): 196–222.

Charlier, R.H., and M.P. Chaineux. 2009. "The Healing Sea: A Sustainable Coastal Ocean Resource: Thalassotherapy." *Journal of Coastal Research* 25 (4): 838–56. https://doi.org/10.2112/08A-0008.1.

Conklin, B., and L. Graham. 1995. "The Shifting Middle Ground: Amazonian Indians and Eco-Politics." *American Anthropologist* 97 (4): 695–710. https://doi.org/10.1525/aa.1995.97.4.02a00120.

Conquest, R. 1986. *The Harvest of Sorrow: Soviet Collectivization and the Terror-Famine.* Oxford: Oxford University Press.

Cracraft, J. 1988. *The Petrine Revolution in Russian Architecture.* Chicago: University of Chicago Press.

Davidov, V. 2013. *Ecotourism and Cultural Production: An Anthropology of Indigenous Spaces in Ecuador.* New York: Palgrave. https://doi.org/10.1057/9781137355386.

Descola, P. 2012. "Beyond Nature and Culture: The Traffic of Souls." *HAU* 2 (1): 473–500. https://doi.org/10.14318/hau2.1.021.

Fausto, C. 2012. "Too Many Owners: Mastery and Ownership in Amazonia." In *Animism in Rainforest and Tundra: Personhood, Animals, Plants and Things in Contemporary Amazonia and Siberia*, edited by M. Brightman, V.E. Grotti, and O. Ulturgasheva, 29–47. Oxford; New York: Berghahn Books.

Fein, J. 2013. "Science and the Sacred in Buddhist Buryatia: The Politics of Chita's Museum-Temple, 1899–1914." *Ab Imperio* 2 (2013): 137–64. https://doi.org/10.1353/imp.2013.0035.

Figes, O. 1997. "The Russian Revolution of 1917 and Its Language in the Village." *Russian Review* 56 (3): 323–45. https://doi.org/10.2307/131747.

Forrester, S. 2006. "Margaret Paxson. *Solovyovo: The Story of Memory in a Russian Village.*" *Folklorica* 11: 123–35. https://doi.org/10.17161/folklorica.v11i0.3777.

Geertz, C. 1973. *The Interretation of Cultures.* New York: Basic Books.

Grandstaff, P.J. 1980. *Interregional Migration in the U.S.S.R.: Economic Aspects, 1959–1970.* Durham, NC: Duke University Press.

Grant, B. 1995. *In the Soviet House of Culture: A Century of Perestroikas.* Princeton: Princeton University Press.

Grenoble, L. 2006. *Language Policy in the Soviet Union*. Dordrecht, Netherlands: Kluwer Academic Publishers.

Heikkinen, K. 2006. "Vepsskaya bob—xranitelnitsa tsensnostey ili otstalosti. Novoe prochtenie polevyx materyalov." In *Sovremennaya Nauka o Vepsax: Dostizheniya I Perspektivi*, edited by I. Vinokurova, 329–47. Petrozavodsk: Karelian Research Centre.

Henry, L., and V. Douhovnikoff. 2008. "Environmental Issues in Russia." *Annual Review of Environment and Resources* 33 (1): 437–60. https://doi.org/10.1146/annurev.environ.33.051007.082437.

Hentilä, S. 1999. "From Independence to the End of the Continuation War, 1917–1944." In *Grand Duchy to Modern State: A Political History of Finland Since 1809*, edited by O. Jussila, S. Hentilä, and J. Nevakivi, 101–213. London: Hurst.

Hessler, J. 2004. *A Social History of Soviet Trade: Trade Policy, Retail Practices, and Consumption, 1917–1953*. Princeton: Princeton University Press.

Ingold, T. 1986. *The Appropriation of Nature: Essays on Human Ecology and Social Relations*. Manchester: Manchester University Press.

Korolkova, L. n.d. "Religious Ideas of the Vepsians: The Role of Orthodoxy in the Life of the Population." Accessed August 15, 2016. http://www.ethnomuseum.ru/religioznye-predstavleniya-vepsov.

Kreps, C. 1998. "Museum-Making and Indigenous Curation in Central Kalimantan, Indonesia." *Museum Anthropology* 22 (1): 5–17. https://doi.org/10.1525/mua.1998.22.1.5.

Kristensen, B. 2007. "The Human Perspective." *Inner Asia* 9 (2): 275–89. https://doi.org/10.1163/146481707793646467.

Kurs, O. 2001. "The Vepsians: An Administratively Divided Nationality." *Nationalities Papers: The Journal of Nationalism and Ethnicity* 29 (1): 69–83. https://doi.org/10.1080/00905990120036385.

Lonin, R. 2000. *Zapiski Kraeveda*. Petrozavodsk: Muzeynoe Agenstvo.

Lonin, R. 2004a. *Zhivet v Narode Pamyat'*. Petrozavodsk: Folium.

Lonin, R. 2004b. *Detstvo Opalennoye Voynoy*. Petrozavodsk: Verso.

Martin, T. 2001. "An Affirmative Action Empire: The Soviet Union as the Highest Form of Imperialism." In *A State of Nations: Empire and Nation-Making in the Age of Lenin and Stalin*, edited by R. Suny and T. Martin, 67–92. New York: Oxford University Press.

Marx, K. 1992. *Capital*, vol. 1, *A Critique of Political Economy*, translated by B. Fowkes. 1867. Reprint, London: Penguin Classics.

Menshenin, A. 2000. Pastuxi i pastusheskaya magiya Karel I Vepsov. Tezisi dokladov 4oy ezhegodnoy nauchnoysStudencheskoj konferentsii aspirantov

I sudentov/Karel'skiy Filial Severno-Zapadnoy Akademii Gosudarstvennoy Sluzhbi. http://gov.karelia.ru/Different/300/confer/docum11.shtml.

Oushakine, S.A. (2007). "We're Nostalgic But We're Not Crazy": Retrofitting the Past in Russia. *The Russian Review* 66 (3): 451–82.

Patico, J. 2000. "'New Russian' Sightings and the Question of Social Difference in St. Petersburg." *Anthropology of East Europe Review* 18 (2): 73–7.

Pedersen, M. 2007. "Multiplicity without Myth: Theorising Darhad Perspectivism." *Inner Asia* 9 (2): 311–28. https://doi.org/10.1163/146481707793646485.

Purzycki, B. 2010. "Spirit Masters, Ritual Cairns, and the Adaptive Religious System in Tyva." *Sibirica* 9 (2): 21–47. https://doi.org/10.3167/sib.2010.090202.

Reeves, M. 2007. "Travels in the Margins of the State: Everyday Geography in the Ferghana Valley Borderlands." In *Everyday Life in Central Asia: Past and Present*, edited by J. Sahadeo and R. Zanca, 281–300. Bloomington: Indiana University Press.

Rogers, D. 2006. "How to Be a Khozyain in a Transforming State: State Formation and the Ethics of Governance in Post-Soviet Russia." *Comparative Studies in Society and History* 48 (04): 915–65. https://doi.org/10.1017/S001041750600034X.

Semakova, I.B., and V.V. Rogozina. 2006. "Materyali po Traditsionnoy Medetsine Vepsov (Mifologicheskiy Aspekt)." In *Sovremennaya Nauka o Vepsax: Dostizheniya I Perspektivi*, edited by I. Vinokurova, 302–14. Petrozavodsk: Karelian Research Centre.

Shearer, D.R. 2006. "Stalinism. 1928–1940." In *The Cambridge History of Russia*, vol. 3, *The Twentieth Century*, edited by R.G. Suny, 192–216. Cambridge: Cambridge University Press. https://doi.org/10.1017/CHOL9780521811446.009.

Siragusa, Laura. 2012. "Vepsian Language: Speaking and Writing Heritage Language in Villages and Cities." PhD diss., University of Aberdeen.

Smith, J. 1999. *The Bolsheviks and the National Question 1917–1923*. London: Macmillan.

Southworth, C. 2006. "The Dacha Debate: Household Agriculture and Labor Markets in Post-Socialist Russia." *Rural Sociology* 71 (3): 451–78. https://doi.org/10.1526/003601106778070671.

Ssorin-Chaikov, N. 2003. *The Social Life of the State in Subarctic Siberia*. Stanford: Stanford University Press.

Stalin, J. 1913. "Marxism and the National Question." *Prosveshcheniye* 3–5. Marxists Internet Archive. https://www.marxists.org/reference/archive/stalin/works/1913/03a.htm.

Stammler, F. 2011. "Oil without Conflict? The Anthropology of Industrialization in Northern Russia." In *Crude Domination: An Anthropology of Oil*, edited by A. Behrendts, S. Reyna, and G. Schlee, 243–69. Oxford; New York: Berghahn Books.

Strogalshikova, Z. 2008a. *Ethnodemographic Processes of Finno-Ugric Peoples of Russia: Primary Tendencies.* // Finno—Ugric Peoples of Russia: Yesterday. Today. Syktyvkdr.

Strogalshikova, Z. 2008b. *Vepsy: na rubezhe XX–XXI vekov.* Petrozavodsk: Rossiyskaya Akademia Nauk, Karel'skij Nauchniy Tsentr. Syktyvkdr.

Tishkov, V. 1997. *The Mind Aflame: Ethnicity, Nationalism and Conflict in and after the Soviet Union.* London: Sage. https://doi.org/10.4135/9781446279427.

Turner, T. 1995. "An Indigenous People's Struggle for Socially Equitable and Ecologically Sustainable Production: The Kayapo Revolt against Extractivism." *Journal of Latin American Anthropology* 1 (1): 98–121.

Verigin, S.G. 2009 "National Policy of the Finnish Government on the Occupied Territory of Karelia in 1941–1944." *RUDN Journal of Russian History* 4 (2009): 5–19.

Vilén, T. 2013. "Studying (and Not Studying) One's Neighbour: Sovietology in Cold War Finland." *Valahian Journal of Historical Studies* 20 (Winter): 73–87.

Vinokurova I.Y. 1989. "Vepsskie Zavetnye Prazdniki Oxrani Skota." In *Problemi Istorii I Kul'turi Vepsskoy Natsional'nosti*, edited by V. Pimenov, 119–30. Petrozavodsk: Petrozavodsk Press.

Vinokurova, I.Y. 2003. "Mifologiya i Verovaniya." In *Pribaltiysko-Finskie Narody Rossii*, edited by E.I. Klementyev and N.V. Shygina, 426–36. Moscow: Nauka.

Vinokurova, I.Y. 2006a. *Zhivotnye v Traditsionnom Milovozzrenii Vepsov.* Petrozavodsk: PetrGU.

Vinokurova, I.Y. 2006b. "Vepsskie Vodyanye Duhi (k rekonstruktsii nekotoryx mifologicheskix predstavlyeniy)." In *Sovremennaya Nauka o Vepsax: Dostizheniya i Perspektivi—Pamyati N. Bogdanova*, edited by N. Bogdanov and I. Vinokurova, 314–28. Petrozavodsk: Rossiyskaya Akademia Nauk, Karel'skij Nauchniy Tsentr.

Volfson, I., Farrakhov, E., Pronin, A., Beiseyev, O., Beiseyev, A., Bogdasarov, M., Oderora, A., Pechenkin, I., Khitrov, A., and Pikhur, O. (2010) *Medical Geology: International Year of Planet Earth.* Springer: Netherlands.

Walker, H. (2012). "Demonic Trade: Debt, Materiality, and Agency in Amazonia." *Journal of the Royal Anthropological Institute* 18 (1): 140–59.

Zaytseva, N.G. n.d. "Vepsian Language Corpus." http://vepsian.krc.karelia.ru/about/.

INDEX

Lightning Source UK Ltd.
Milton Keynes UK
UKHW010604071119
353068UK00010B/156/P